The
Year
of the
Poet XII

December 2025

The Poetry Posse

inner child press, ltd.
'building bridges of cultural understanding'

The Poetry Posse 2025

Gail Weston Shazor

Shareef Abdur Rasheed

Teresa E. Gallion

hülya n. yılmaz

Noreen Snyder

Tzemin Ition Tsai

Elizabeth Esguerra Castillo

Jackie Davis Allen

Mutawaf Shaheed

Caroline 'Ceri' Nazareno

Ashok K. Bhargava

Alicja Maria Kuberska

Swapna Behera

Albert 'Infinite' Carrasco

Kimberly Burnham

Eliza Segiet

William S. Peters, Sr.

~ * ~

In order to maintain each poet's authentic voice, this volume has not undergone the scrutiny of editing. Please take time to indulge each contributor for their own creativity and aspirations to convey their uniqueness.

hülya n. yılmaz, Ph.D.
Director of Editing ~
Inner Child Press International

The Year of the Poet XII
December 2025 Edition

The Poetry Posse

1st Edition : 2025

This Publishing is protected under Copyright Law as a "Collection". All rights for all submissions are retained by the Individual Author and or Artist. No part of this Publishing may be Reproduced, Transferred in any manner without the prior **WRITTEN CONSENT** of the "Material Owners" or its Representative Inner Child Press. Any such violation infringes upon the Creative and Intellectual Property of the Owner pursuant to International and Federal Copyright Laws. Any queries pertaining to this "Collection" should be addressed to Publisher of Record.

Publisher Information

1st Edition : Inner Child Press
intouch@innerchildpress.com
www.innerchildpress.com

Copyright © 2025 : The Poetry Posse

ISBN-13 : 978-1-961498-77-8 (inner child press, ltd.)

$ 12.99

WHAT WOULD LIFE BE WITHOUT A LITTLE POETRY?

Dedication

This Book is dedicated to

Humanity, Peace & Poetry

the Power of the Pen

can effectuate change!

&

The Poetry Posse

past, present & future,

our Patrons and Readers &

the Spirit of our Everlasting Muse

In the darkness of my life
I heard the music
I danced . . .
and the Light appeared
and I dance

Janet P. Caldwell

Table of Contents

The Poetry Posse

Table of Contents . . . *continued*

December's Featured Poets   107

Inner Child Press News   141

Other Anthological Works   185

Foreword

Transcendence ~ Legacy ~ Satisfaction

Once again, we have come to yet another year-end with our monthly publication. The Poetry Posse and our featured poets have been making this monthly anthology, *The Year of the Poet,* possible since 2014 without any interruption along the way. After 12 years, we continue to be elated in our contributions from various parts of the world to the genre of poetry.

"Transcendence, Legacy" and "Satisfaction" are the focal themes in this 44th issue. In this past year, our thematic foci have varied between anxiety, peacefulness, grief, isolation, empowerment, confusion, love, gratitude, contentment, innocence, joy, and longing, to list only a few. We have all done our diligent research on each of the themes in order to gain better insight into the highlighted human condition and emotions, and to modestly offer our readership the same glimpses.

We hope that this final issue of the year 2025 will help us all to not only briefly visit the concepts of transcendence, legacy, and satisfaction as another set of 12 months come to an end, but also to further contemplate these conceptualizations of human life.

hülya n. yılmaz, Ph.D.

Now Open for Submissions

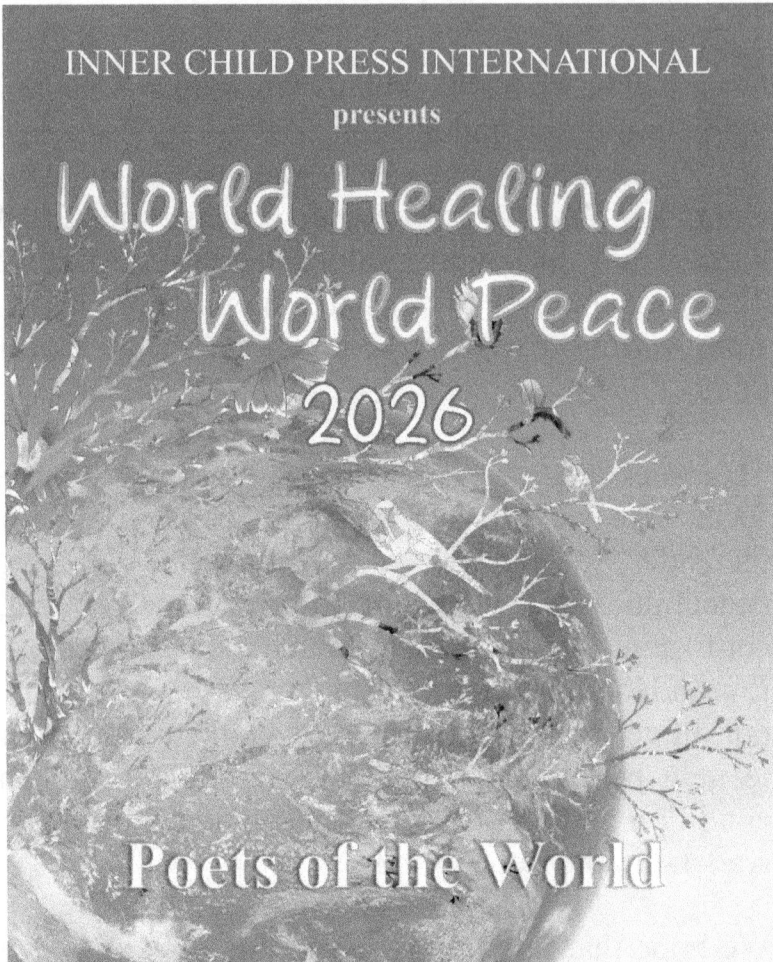

INNER CHILD PRESS INTERNATIONAL

presents

World Healing World Peace

2026

Poets of the World

Submit to :

worldhealingworldpeace@gmail.com

x

Preface

We, **Inner Child Press International, The Year of the Poet** and **The Poetry Posse** welcome you.

As we now at the end of our 12th year of monthly publications for **The Year of the Poet**, we still continue to be excited.

This coming year of 2026, our themes will be civilizations. As we month by month poetically explore many current and psat cultures, I hope you will join us.

For those of you who are not familiar with our story, back in 2013, a few of us poets got together with the simple intention of producing a book a month. That was our challenge. Since that time the enterprise has blossomed and brought forth a fruit that seems to keep on growing as evidenced as we enter 2023.

Our purpose is simple. Through our lyrical words and verse, we not only wish to share our poetic works, but we also have the poetic naiveté to believe that we can assist in the growth of consciousness of the things that have an effect our collective humanity. Therefore, we welcome your readership. For more about what we are attempting to accomplish, have a look at our Publishing Web Site . . . www.innerchildpress.com. If you would like to

know a bit more about this particular endeavor please stop by for a visit at :
www.innerchildpress.com/the-year-of-the-poet

Over the years, Inner Child Press has been socially active to bring awareness and catalog through literature the things that have an impact upon our world and its inhabitants. We have solicited, produced, underwritten and published quite a few volumes to that end. For more insight you may wish to visit : www.innerchildpress.com/the-anthology-market. If you are a writer, poet, or activist, you would be advised to keep a eye out for upcoming volumes should you desire to participate. All readers are welcomed as well. Note, that there is a myriad of published volumes that are available as a FREE PDF download as well as available for purchase at affordable prices.

We at this time extend to you our well wishes for your own personal journey and hope that you consider including us as a travel companion.

Bless Up

Bill

William S. Peters, Sr.

Publisher
Inner Child Press International
www.innerchildpress.com

Transcendence ~ Legacy ~ Satisfaction

Water Lily   Forget-me-nots   Daisies

This last month of 2025 we discuss our sense of Transcendence, moments of profound clarity and connection; Legacy, contemplating the impact and meaning of one's life; and Satisfaction, a feeling of completeness and harmony with life. These weeks before New Year's on the darkest days of the year, are a great time, no matter our age to think about what we are grateful for and what we leave behind each day as we go to sleep and what we will be remembered for when we are no longer here.

Contemplating beauty, poet, Alfred K. LaMotte expressed, "Beauty unfolds in the silence between thoughts. The dark loam of thought-free awareness is where words of creation spring up and cry, "Let there be light." Creation is neither a tale of the past nor a vision of the future, but a history of this moment. That is why, for me, meditation is the mother of poetry."

Consider what springs up for you as you read these poems?

In *Praying*, Mary Oliver notes, "It doesn't have to be the blue iris, it could be weeds in a vacant lot, or a few small stones; just pay attention, then patch a few words together and don't try to make them elaborate, this isn't a contest but the doorway into thanks, and a silence in which another voice may speak."

Are you a good listener or are you just waiting for your turn to talk?

What are doorways of thanks for you? What comes out of the silence?

Joyce Sutphen contemplates the reasons why someone might leave the country of their birth and express gratitude for a new place in *Sometimes Never* saying, "Talking, we begin to find the way into our hearts, we who knew no words, words being a rare commodity in those countries we left behind. Both refugees and similarly deprived, we marvel at the many things there are to say: so many variations and colors of the same thought, so many different lengths in the words that line up together on our tongues. No scarcity, no rationing, no waiting in line in order to buy."

Each day is a new place to give our input, thoughts, and love. What is the legacy you leave each day or expect to leave when you are gone from this world?

Kimberly Burnham, PhD
(Integrative Medicine)
September, 2025 Spokane, WA & Portland, OR

Poets . . .
sowing seeds in the
Conscious Garden of Life,
that those who have yet to come
may enjoy the Flowers.

Poets, Writers . . . know that we are the enchanting magicians that nourishes the seeds of dreams and thoughts . . . it is our words that entice the hearts and minds of others to believe there is something grand about the possibilities that life has to offer and our words tease it forth into action . . . for you are the Poet, the Writer to whom the Gift of Words has been entrusted . . .

~ wsp

poetry is . . .

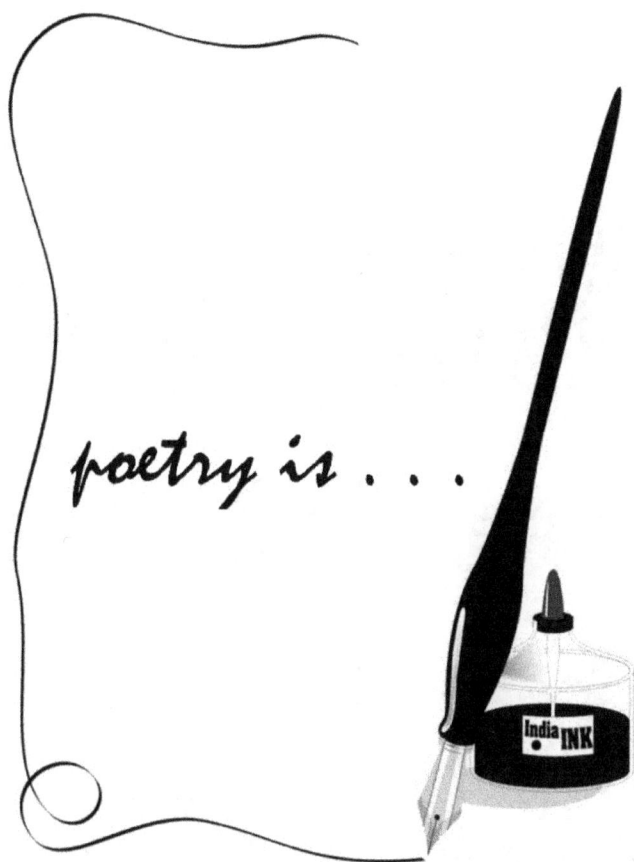

Poetry succeeds where instruction fails.

~ wsp

Open for Submissions

Open until December 31st

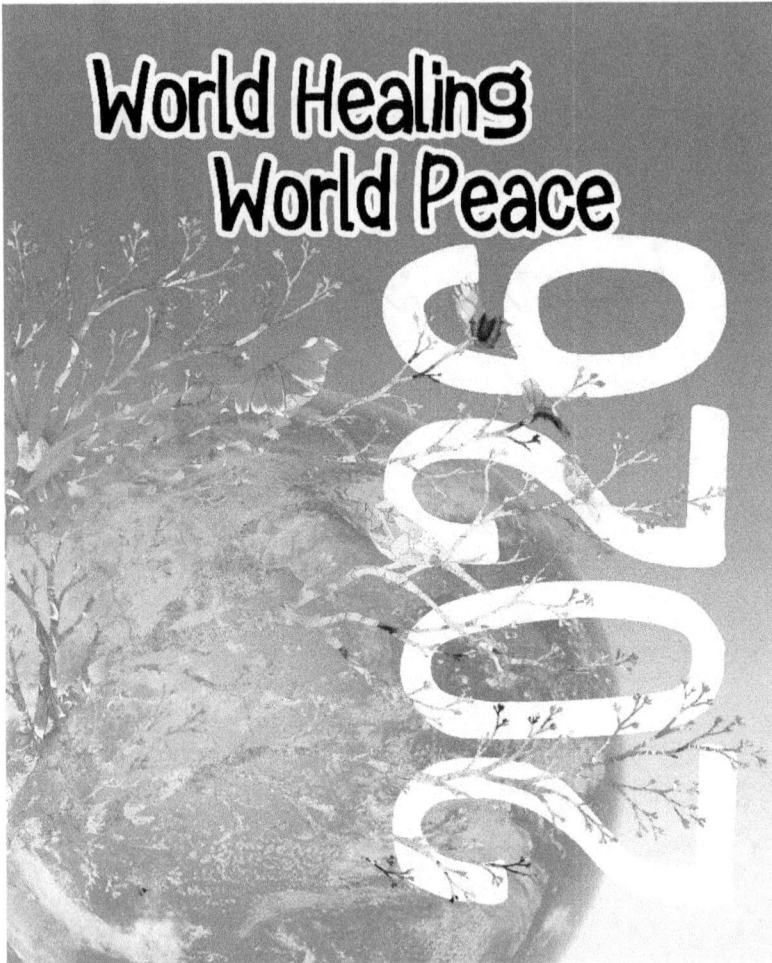

worldhealingworldpeace@gmail.com

A Few Words...... Jackie Davis Allen

My life is and has been a gift, surviving childhood not promised, other than in the prognosis, " She's too ornery to die".

The days were long, the months longer, stretching into the next year. The hospital had become my home.

My would-be third-grade class-mates were busy practicing cursive writing. The "ornery" part of me, assuming creative license, confiscated misplaced, hypodermic needles. With them, I played nurse to my baby doll. Until the doctor of my prognosis, organized a search party and found me out.

I secretly called him "Dr Brassiere". Unable to pronounce his given name, I had overheard him talking to my parents, saying he agreed with the medical staff: "she has but a 50-50 chance of survival".

With more than a half century now behind me, I decided, in 2024, that it was time to return to my art and spend 2025 at my easel. To that end, I submitted all of my poems to the 2025 edition of The Year of the Poet a year in advance!

However, 2025 had other plans in store for me. None of them included art. Instead, Covid-19, pneumonia, hospitalizations, setbacks, for both my husband and me, along with regaining strength have been, and most recently continue to highlight and lowlight my days. Even still, I've set a goal for 2026, when I'll be taking a sabbatical from The Year of the Poet. It is during this time I'll be working on my 4th collection of poetry!

To William S. Peters, Sr, my dear friend and publisher, I thank you for having opened the door to what has been more than eleven years of the most amazing, creative and richly satisfying chapters of my life.

I'd be remiss not to say, to my dear editor, Hulya N Yilmaz and our fellow Poetry Posse poets, it has been both an honor and a pleasure being a part of this esteemed group.

And, as the saying goes, in the Cumberland Mountains of Appalachia, where I grew up, I will be back! "God willin, and iffen the creek don't rize"!

Jackie Davis Allen

Gail Weston Shazor

Gail Weston Shazor

Gail Weston Shazor is a lover of words. She is fond of the arcane, unusual and the not yet words.

Coining words at an early age, there was often a bit of trouble with teachers, but she always had her mother and aunt to back up her choices in expression. Born in Mississippi, she spent her early years with her grandparents. Each of the four left very careful influences on her pre-schooling. She learned in turn how women worked in and out of the home and how men worked in and out of the home to support the family. She learned that a lack of proper schooling was not the only way to learn and understanding life was a great teacher. As in most rural families of color, women had a greater chance of formal learning. Both of Gail's grandmothers read out loud to the family whether it was the bible or the newspapers and important documents to their spouses.

Gail Weston Shazor has authored (so far) Notes from the Blue Roof, A Overstanding of an Imperfect Love, HeartSongs and Lies My Grandfather's Told Me. The number of anthologies is too many to list with the premier accomplishment of one of the contributors to The Year of The Poet. Gail will always lend her ink to community projects and will purchase the books of fellow poets in the Inner Child Press family.

making it

The way you make love is the way God will be with you.
(Rumi)

I need to hold your hand
To feel your fingers intertwined
Into mine
Holding my palm close to yours
Lifeline to fingerprint
Pull me gently into your chest
So I can feel you breathe
The rise and fall
Comforts the threadbare places
The spaces where pride
Has leaked out onto my lap
I need you to patch them
As you bite my neck
Possessively with gentle power
To mold this dry clay into
Something malleable
Tasty and I dare say, pretty
Because I need you to
Really see me as I want to be
Wanted
This is how you can
Make love with me
Fully dressed and stretched out
Alongside you, barely touching
And yet held fully
Completely, unconditionally
I need you to love me
As if I was fashioned by your hands
For then we both become
The created

Disremebered

I lost the title in my thoughts
So jumbled together as they were
Fleeting around the edges
Of memories, old, new and coming
Gone are the days
That we separated each other
By skin color
And when my generation dies
You will have to find colorism in a book
There is no forbidden love
No love that we have to be jailed for possessing
I can remember being bi-colored
High Yellow
Mullato
Mixed Race
And I only think on bears now
Would I fear a polar bear more than a brown bear?
Are my white relatives to be feared
More than my black or
My Indian tribe,
I don't think so
I wonder if sisters on each side
Of the Berlin Wall would genetically change
To enemies
Or did the Tutsis gain education because
They favored the Belgians more in complexion
Than the Hutus
All sharing a common language
For thousands of years with the TWA people
Why is a house slave better
Then a yard slave
Or a field slave
800,000 rumors on African soil

1 little girl on Mississippi soil
Who has never seen a bear free
Taught that life labeled dangerous
Had to be caged
And still clinging to the thought
Of Native ancestors that all life
Is cherished life
I drink water now
And ponder on the life that calls to me
From the margins
Jumbled together as they are
Whispering to be heard
This started as a Happy Mother's day piece
And so it goes
All women are wisdom bearers
And they exist to share the knowledge
Whether actively birthing or not
As they teach the children
All children
To see life
Question life
And protect life
So bears can continue to exist
Free
So we can continue to exist
Without labels
Free

Wristwatch

Hopeful
Here
I am though
Lost remain
Faded ribbons
Black on navy
Lost you with life
Shelves dusty on
Gifts kept
Life tuned in itself
Sadness of passing
Keep creep time
~Wristwatch~
Time creep keep
Passing of sadness
Itself in tuned life
Kept gifts
On dusty shelves
Life with you lost
Navy on black
Ribbons faded
Remain lost
Though i am
Here
Hopeful

Alicja Maria Kuberska

Alicja Maria Kuberska

Alicja Maria Kuberska – awarded Polish poetess, novelist, journalist, editor.

She is a member of the Polish Writers Associations in Warsaw, Poland and IWA Bogdani, Albania. She is also a member of directors' board of Soflay Literature Foundation, Our Poetry Archive (India) and Cultural Ambassador for Poland (Inner Child Press, USA)

Her poems have been published in numerous anthologies and magazines in : Poland, Czech Republic, Slovakia, Hungary,Ukraina, Belgium, Bulgaria, Albania, Spain, the UK, Italy, the USA, Canada, the UK, Argentina, Chile, Peru, Israel, Turkey, India, Uzbekistan, South Korea, Taiwan, China, Australia, South Africa, Zambia, Nigeria

She received two medals - the Nosside UNESCO Competition in Italy (2015) and European Academy of Science Arts and Letters in France (2017). Ahe also received a reward of international literary competition in Italy „ Tra le parole e 'elfinito" (2018). She was announced a poet of the 2017 year by Soflay Literature Foundation (2018).She also received : Bolesław Prus Prize Poland (2019), Culture Animator Poland (2019) and first prize Premio Internazionale di Poesia Poseidonia- Paestrum Italy (2019).

Transcendence

Letting go of emotion is never easy,
nor is forgetting the pull of desire,
clearing the mind of its restless storm
and gazing inward.
There, in that quiet depth,
one may find the first light—
a radiance that shines upon
the tree of knowledge of good and evil,
whispering that love is the only thing
that truly endures.
No one will remember
the brand of your car,
the color of your walls,
the tags sewn into your clothing.
The scent of costly perfume will vanish;
everything will crumble into dust.
But someone, years from now, may recall
a smile you once offered,
a few words of comfort,
a handful of coins pressed into a palm,
the warmth of a handshake, a fleeting kiss.
These things—
insignificant yet essential,
without price yet priceless—
carry a person's memory
into eternity.

Poetry

Poetry, tell me—along which path
will you guide my steps?
Will you reveal the legacy you guard?
Shall I wander through a graveyard of thoughts,
where unborn words died upon empty pages,
where no consonant, no vowel ever rose to speak,
and the blankness froze emotions
before they had a chance to breathe?
Or will you lead me through a garden instead—
a place blooming with metaphors and comparisons,
where words unfurl like petals
or spill across the page
like a waterfall in motion?
Between being and non-being lies
a narrow, fragile border
I cross again and again
in search of your beauty,
O poetry.

Satisfaction

It takes many years to understand
that life rarely grants us grand events,
and that the quiet moments, small and fleeting,
hold a charm of their own.
Time will race forward, refusing
to give us back what it has taken.
A child's smile, tiny hands
will grow into a thoughtful gaze
and a firm, adult grip.
In the mirror, the reflection will fade.
The lovely girl and the handsome boy
will disappear,
and the old will limp slowly
toward their fate.
It is not worth waiting only
for Sundays and holidays—
that is merely waiting for the death
of all the other days
of the week.

you with it, Mom.

Jackie Davis Allen

Jackie Davis Allen

Jackie Davis Allen, otherwise known as Jacqueline D. Allen or Jackie Allen, grew up in the Cumberland Mountains of Appalachia. As the next eldest daughter of a coal miner father and a stay at home mother, she was the first in her family to attend and graduate from college. Her siblings, in their own right, are accomplished, though she is the only one, to date, that has discovered the gift of writing.

Graduating from Radford University, with a Bachelor's of Science degree in Early Education, she taught in both public and private schools. For over a decade she taught private art classes to children both in her home and at a local Art and Framing Shop where she also sold her original soft sculptured Victorian dolls and original christening gowns.

She resides in northern Virginia with her husband, taking much needed get-aways to their mountain home near the Blue Ridge Mountains, a place that evokes memories of days spent growing up in the Appalachian Mountains.

A lover of hats, she has worn many. Following marriage to her college sweetheart, and as wife, mother, grandmother, teacher, tutor, artist, writer, poet and crafter, she is a lover of art and antiques, surrounding herself, always, with books, seeking to learn more.

In 2015 she authored *Looking for Rainbows, Poetry, Prose and Art*, and in 2017, *Dark Side of the Moon*. Both books of mostly narrative poetry were published by Inner Child Press and were edited by hulya n. yilmaz in 2019, *No Illusions. Through the Looking Glass*, which was nominated to be considered for a Pulitzer Prize by the publisher and editor of Inner Child Press, ltd.

http://www.innerchildpress.com/jackie-davis-allen.php
jackiedavisallen.com

Transcendence

Were sufficient words, at my disposal,

And I competently erudite to explain,
I'd heap compliments upon the heads
Of my friends, too numerous to name.

Had I been wiser, in youthful days,

Maybe I'd have understood, that pain
Welcomes empathy, compassion;
That humility has no need for blame.

In long-past-days of innocence,

I toyed with emotions, played games.
Today I've no need for pretension's sake.
I'm older, happy, uninterested in fame.

Sweet rose garden, I inhale your beauty.

I love your sunny fragrance, and claim
Blue skies above. Call me Satisfied,
My legacy defines what remains.

God's mercy has gifted me with talent.

He has allowed me to transcend great pain.
Gratefully, I share the gifts I've received.
And, that without an ounce of shame.

Legacy

"Something to do with art."

I responded to a question whose meaning
Was beyond my understanding. The world
Not yet open, unavailable to my cloistered life.
A childhood dream, laid aside. Held hostage
By poverty's painful, and virtual penury.

Decades behind others, in experience,
Hungrier than many, my dreams were just that.
I found education's path held opportunities,
Beyond those available in the Cumberland
Mountains of Appalachia. Where I was born.

Never one to give up, many times I felt
That situations in which I found myself,
Had master manipulators controlling
The puppet strings. With me as the puppet.
My own mind filled with self-determination.

Guided by God's great goodness, spared
Consequences I deserved, given life, with
Diagnosis to the contrary, I've discovered
Riches-untold have fallen into my lap.
Not the customary wealth like gems or gold.

What legacy I leave behind will find itself
Manifested in family, in friendships made.
In tangible pieces of creativity, whether
Paintings, poetry, or found treasures.
Like antiques, quilts, china, books, photos.

I've a grateful heart, for a beloved husband.
Devoted children. For a union that's spanned
More than a half century. My cup runs over.
I pray yours does too.

Satisfaction

There's a song in the air.

Simple things make me happy!
A good book of poetry, a friend's or mine;
Music. Paintings, sculpture, antiques, rugs.
Flowers. A little wine. They need not cost
A lot or be expensive. Only well loved!

The fireplace is blazing.

I'm cozied up in my recliner, my husband
Across the room, in his identical chair.
Light turquoise-blue, leather, complimenting
The colors in the Persian rug. Lying beneath.
Purchased for a song from serendipity's eye.

A Pakistani throw smiles up at me.

I'm the Queen of Green, my roots cultivated
In the soil of thriftiness that has been handed
Down by ancestors' desire for artistic style.
Having lunch at an aunt's home, using silver
Flatware, with crystal handles. In my dreams.

A velvet party gown hangs in my closet.

Fights over hand-me-downs, resolved easily,
Just tuck it beneath one arm, like my sisters!
What we did, when the "mother-lode" arrived.
A note of caution: "Hand-me-downs," was not
In our vocabulary! Instead, "Haute couture!"

I am blessed! I am loved!

I'm satisfied with my life! Yet, would be happier
Were my health's wealth not on the wane.
I've experienced some highs in life. Some lows.
I've been hungry, thirsty. But I've overcome
The hurdles to where I am! Thanks be to God!

Tzemin
Ition
Tsai

Dr. Tzemin Ition Tsai comes from the Republic of China(Taiwan). In addition to being a professor of literature at a university, he is more committed to writing poems, novels, and proses. He is also an editor of "Reading, Writing and Teaching" academic text, an International editor of "Contemporary dialogues" literary periodical in Macedonia, and Vice-Chairman of the International Jury of the SAHITTO INTERNATIONAL AWARD in Bangladesh, and a columnist for "Chinese Language Monthly" in Taiwan.

In a wide range of literary creations, he is particularly fond of interesting stories or novels, and writing articles or poems about the feelings of nature and human beings. He has won many national literary awards. His literary works have been anthologized and published in books, journals, and newspapers in more than 55 countries and have been translated into more than 24 languages.

Crossing Mountains, a Heart Unmoved

I was a small child, treading the narrow ridge between the fields;
morning smoke from the kitchen rose unhurried,
turning yesterday's dreams
into the fragrance of rice upon the table.
A bowl of clear porridge kept quiet company with the ancestral tablets,
beside them a single thread of fading incense.

Blessings, you said, are not begged from heaven alone;
you must steady your own chopsticks if you wish the rice to last.
For a slight yet stubborn wish, I clenched my teeth
and on the waiting page scratched out one fragile line, my name.

My fingers trembled like autumn's final leaf.
The oil lamp slid a little closer, silently;
the mountain road was steep, and the human heart
no wider than a palm, let one thought stray,
and the level path falls away into ravine.
Beyond the house, that long, unbroken chain of hills
was a lifetime of kindness and of debt I could never fully cross.
To climb a mountain is never to stand upon another's head;
it is simply to cease losing to the nights that once filled you with fear.

I came at last to the loneliest stretch of road,
murmuring your stern old sentences like charms against the dark.
With a pack on my back I stepped over the village's aging bridge;

you pressed a rusted ring of keys into my hand, softly
reminding me
to remember the way home.

Now I walk the mountain roads of others, and suddenly you
return to me,
the figure straightening up among the grain.
After every fall, it is always you who rises in my heart:
the one who taught me how to cross mountains without
letting the heart be moved.

Old Tiles Passing On the Light

Tier upon tier of old tiles press down an alley of years.
Each day the kitchen smoke ascends, warming the morning
from within.
By the well-rail, a wooden bucket waits forever for a pair
of hands.
On the door-lintel, old couplets still cling, their strokes
worn soft by the wind.
Grandfather sits in his bamboo chair, old calluses resting in
his palms.
He says, A person must be deep and thick, like the soil of
this courtyard,
plowed once in spring, once in autumn, and still it raises
grain and weeds.

Grandmother polishes a bowl until it shines like a single
moon.
She says, Not a grain of rice should be spared;
what you leave in the bowl will ripen into sighs.
I lower my eyes to the bowl, then lift them to her lined
face.
On the table, an old teapot, its spout chipped at the lip;
yet the tea within stays hot, like warnings that never run
dry.
My schoolbag leans in the corner, silently reciting every
lesson,
while my dream hides in the crease of a dog-eared page.

I long to walk beyond the village gate, past every
whispered prayer,
to be one who lives by words, gathering all they cannot say
and, stroke by stroke, writing them larger, writing them
bright.

The rainy season comes and goes; from the seams between
the tiles
small grasses push their way up, each blade climbing, never
bending down.
I learn from them, setting my fallen days in a single row,
and treading on them, one by one, as a new flight of steps.

Where Time Builds a Nation

Look,
the Great Wall winding across a thousand miles,
not mere stones upon stones,
but countless hands,
frost and storm hardened into veins of steel.
Look,
the Yellow River surges,
its muddy waves thunder with the chest of the ancients.
Though for a thousand years it changes its course,
it never surrenders its rush toward the sea.
From bamboo slips to paper scrolls,
from paper scrolls to lamplight study,
the brush has carved more than words,
it has etched the unyielding marrow
of a people unbroken.
Mountains rise, rivers fall,
and through the vastness of time
the spine remains straight,
like a pine defying snow.
Standing against the wind,
O world, behold!
Here, where time builds layer upon layer,
stands the ancient heart of China.

Noreen Snyder

Noreen Ann Snyder has been writing since she was a teenager. She writes a variety of different topics. Her favorite poetic forms are Sonnets, Blitz, Haiku, Tanka, and Free Verse. She always learning different poetic forms.

Noreen Ann Snyder is a poet, writer, and an author of five books, (four books are co-authored with her late husband, Garry A. Snyder.) Her poetry is in several Inner Child Press Anthologies. She is the founder ofThe Poetry Club on Facebook.

My Legacy

I want to leave behind
my legacy of love,
making a difference
through my poetry,
through how I live.

I want to leave behind
Never give up
keep pushing on.

I want to leave behind
you[re never too old or too young
to live your dreams.

I want to leave behind
God and Jesus are real
Let them in your life

I want to leave behind
love, honesty, loyal and true.
If I have done all these things,
my life has been fulfilled
with happiness and joy.

Honesty

Honesty will get you
far in life.
Honesty will draw
people to you
and see how faithful, loyal
and true you are.

Honesty is like a sunrise.
You know the sunrise will be
there every morning
so faithful.

Without honesty,
who can we trust?
Not a single person!
We need more honesty
in this world.
Life will be that much more
easier in this world.

Just You (Trinet)

Today, tomorrow

Be you

take the mask off of you

Let us see the real person

bare, rawness

not holding back

Just you.

Elizabeth E. Castillo

Elizabeth Esguerra Castillo

Elizabeth Esguerra Castillo is a multi-awarded and an Internationally-Published Contemporary Author/Poet and a Professional Writer / Creative Writer / Feature Writer / Journalist / Travel Writer from the Philippines. She has 2 published books, "Seasons of Emotions" (UK) and "Inner Reflections of the Muse", (USA). Elizabeth is also a co-author to more than 60 international anthologies in the USA, Canada, UK, Romania, India. She is a Contributing Editor of Inner Child Magazine, USA and an Advisory Board Member of Reflection Magazine, an international literary magazine. She is a member of the American Authors Association (AAA) and PEN International.

Web links:

Facebook Fan Page

https://free.facebook.com/ElizabethEsguerraCastillo

Google Plus

https://plus.google.com/u/0/+ElizabethCastillo

The Journey

I rise from the quiet corners of myself,
from the dust of days that once felt heavy—
unfolding like light discovering a crack in the sky.

There is a soft unbinding in the soul
when one chooses to become more than sorrow,
more than memory,
more than the echoes that cling to old rooms of the heart.

I step into the wind without asking its name.
It carries me—
past the edges of what I believed I could be,
past the borders written by fear and forgetting.

To transcend is not to escape,
but to return to the world newly formed,
to breathe with a wider chest,
to see with eyes washed in dawn.

I walk where shadows once held me,
and they bow like tired sentinels
who know their watch is done.

Still, the journey is not an ascent alone—
it is a remembering:
that I was always sky,
always wildfire,
always capable of lifting myself
beyond the gravity of yesterday.

Here, in this quiet rising,
I become the song I once sought—
unbound, unnamed,
and infinite.

Free Spirit

I am a free spirit roaming across the sky
The warm caress of the evening breeze,
Touches my damp, cold skin.
Embracing the seasons as they come rushing in,
A new frontier opens and welcomes every soul
Who dares to enter this hallow space in time.

I am a constant traveler defying rhyme and reason,
A pilgrim rekindling an ancient spell
Waiting for the dawning of a brand new morn
Full of hope, peace, and contentment.

Choose Yourself More

Amidst the chaos, the madness around,

Be the one who inspires

Across a room full of fools

Be the one who radiates peace

After all is said and done,

Be the one who chooses herself more

Rather that staying where you are not celebrated.

Mutawaf Shaheed

Mutawaf Shaheed

C. E. Shy has been writing since the seventh grade. He continued writing through high school, until he became more involved in sports. After his graduation, he worked at the White Motors Company where he wrote for the company's newspaper. He started a column called: "The Poet's Corner." That was his first published work.

www.innerchildpress.com/c-e-shy.php

[EXITS]

The wind swept sea breezes past my nostrils again today.
I watched waves play tag and sea life flourished in front of
me.
My shadow cast itself upon the sands and moved from right
to left
Then left me standing there.
I smell the leaves as they fall. I remember when some of
them bloomed.
A fly sought refuge on my screen hoping not to be seen by
the bird's eye.
The orchestra started up in my head again removing the
taint of ill.

My thoughts ganged up on me freeing them from my pen
displaying
Them selves on the pages below.
The day found it difficult to get through itself until night
fell.
The stars hurried to their positions in the sky; they couldn't
wait to twinkle.
Their light searched for light around each other.
Sun shine and rain drops found their way through cracks in
the green house.
There was a deadly game afoot. The game of hawk and rat
the owl and the mouse.
From the sky to the ground without a sound one less mouse
for grandmas house one
less rat for the cat.

Looking Back

We were the rhythm and rhyme of our time. Your destiny was like mine. Pride was out side. Honesty was blatant. Sometime our thoughts collided. In my head were things like sugar, butter and bread.

Blue things fled across my fore head. My minds eye never lost sight of you. Your kisses were concentrated while the rest of the world was evaporating.

I almost drowned in fantastic. My eyes photographed you standing against the purple landscape.

Everything around us embraced you. The wind delivered your fragrances to me. The application to my skin was easy. We stood inside the minutes waiting for the hours to catch up.

Now seems like then. How do you measure the treasure? The thoughts of you march around in my head keeping me from my sleep. The color of love is clear.

I took a risk and stepped outside of you hoping you wouldn't disappear. I saw my reflection in your eyes. Your eyes sparkled as we sat in slow motion.

Sounds from the ocean organized without time to measure it. There was no clock to stop. You rained in my head. You came to me to me in 4D. I had to come through you to see me.

The Get Away

Words pass me at night trying to find minds to sign on.
I connect to things that my thoughts forgot to mention.
Images lubricated by time decoct and become un-done
with the rising of the sun's shine.
Another day of being pursued by definitions remaining
even unclear to the scribes.
I Find parallels uneven.
I stand stymied by organs playing off key to Chinese
operas.
My daily chores move quickly as I rush back in time.
I orchestrate my momentum to accommodate the changing
vibe.
My mind was sentenced to something less than me.
Humidity played no role in my sweating. My shirt was wet
from
old memories that leaked and things I'm forgetting.
The winds came alive then died because nobody loved
them.
The trees and flowers were confused and began to bloom in
blizzards.
Wizards wrapped in turbans drank old Grand Dad into a
stupor.
Sitting here trying to open mind locks. Rolling dice that
had no sevens
nor elevens, that couldn't even make a point.
I had to get away from the minutia.

hülya
n.
yılmaz

Liberal Arts Professor Emerita, hülya n. yılmaz [sic] is Co-Chair and Director of Editing Services at Inner Child Press International, a published author, ghostwriter, and translator (EN, DE, and TU; in any direction). Her literary contributions appeared in a large number of national and international anthologies.

hülya writes creatively to attain and nourish a comprehensive awareness for and development of our humanity.

hülya n. yılmaz, a traveler on the journey called "life" . . .

Writing Web Site
https://hulyanyilmaz.com/

Editing Web Site
https://hulyasfreelancing.com

transcending death

"Kırık Kanat" was the title of it,
the first book Mom gave us to read.

"The Broken Wing" . . .
about one family's ordeals and
a bird with a broken wing that kept
appearing on the window ledge
of their single-room flat.

The family was living at ground level,
befitting the father's income edge.
Then, a little avian beauty
starts to visit them every day.

I read that magical story again and again.
Have you, by any chance, read it, too?
Mom's copy is with me.
I kept it intact all these long years.

Would she cry as hard now if she knew
how miserably apart you and I grew,
her precious two?

I am different;
that is true.
I walked a path of mess,
hurting family, though with no intent,
honing learned flaws, I would rather live without.
They are, however, not any different from yours.

Not even once have I aimed at not loving you.
I just loved,

respecting,
and admiring you.
I always put you on a pedestal.

But not anymore!
For also the unhurt wing
has now broken from its core.

Nazım's Legacy

The news was impossible for me to disregard,
And regarded, I have.

I, a woman who has long passed her 60s,
Born into modern Turkey before leaving
For the United States of America,
My similarly tainted adoptive country
In pursuit of an advanced academic career
Numerous decades ago.

So,
I have
Resorted
To the infinite
Embrace of ease
And offerings of comfort
That only poetry succeeds to lend.

In my attempt
To at least somewhat forget,
I have called in my all-time favorite poet
To come to my rescue with his worldly work,
And he, the legendary and gracious Nazım Hikmet,
Appeared in my sphere.

Terribly saddened by the latest shock
Toward his utterly beloved country,
The one also of my birth,
I imagined how this world-renowned Turk
Would rest his dire concerns
About Turkey's fate.

Her women had gathered in multiple thousands
For a peaceful protest and marched in Istanbul,
Demanding the enactment of the Child Sex Law.

Nazım's imagined visit
To my library of his books occurred.
Our shared perusal of his poetry
Mirrored his unwavering trust in Turkey's women.
So, I began to feel reassured
Thanks to his prophetic deliberations.
His deeply rooted concerns were still there,
About the long-ago status of Turkish women;
The past wrongdoings will indeed persist. No doubt.
However, as long as the female resistance exists,
Insisted Nazım through his literary excellence,
It will continue to attain a balance
Between evil and good.
There will, therefore, always be
Hope for all humanity
From this point on
To eternity.

prematurely born but . . .

no womb to take the tears to
the hurt is way above you
as you are only half-grown

still, a premature fetal fist
forces to let its presence lurk
inside its three hundred ninety grams of mass
and the mere seven pounds of brain matter
not once, not twice, nor the nth time,
but as a full-grown and content guest in you

Teresa E. Gallion

Teresa E. Gallion is a seeker on a journey to work on unfolding spiritually in this present lifetime. Writing is a spiritual exercise for Teresa. Her passions are traveling the world and hiking the mountain and desert landscapes of the western United States. Her journeys into nature are nurtured by the Sufi poets Rumi and Hafiz. The land is sacred ground and her spiritual temple where she goes for quiet reflection and contemplation. She has published five books: Walking Sacred Ground, Contemplation in the High Desert, Chasing Light, a finalist in the 2013 New Mexico/Arizona Book Awards, Scent of Love, a finalist in the 2021 New Mexico/Arizona Book Awards and Come Egypt in 2024. She has two CDs, *On the Wings of the Wind* and *Poems from Chasing Light*. Her work has appeared in numerous journals and anthologies.

Website: http://teresagallion.yolasite.com/

Transcending

The desert whispers in our ears.
We listen with intention
to honor the message received.

The slow burn in our cheeks
bleed with radiance
from the sun's long reach.

We inhale the gentle breeze
that massages soft lips
ready to express gratitude.

The trees shadow lights
send a welcome song
streaking across the sand.

Between earth and sky
a revolution of joy
dances in predawn light.

We savor our morning flavors
as rain beats a rhythm
that moves the soul forward.

Bubbling in Peacefulness

The annual blessing comes
dressed in golden yellow
with a song singing in the wind.

Between dawn and dusk
the light streams create
a fantasy in yellow bubbles.

Every leaf has a purpose.
Stimulated by the scent of autumn
to put a smile on your face

and whisper in your ear
that winter is coming
to embrace you in love.

The satisfaction of knowing
is elixir for the soul.
Grab and hold tight.

Word Legacy

We do not leave a piece of flesh
painted in fiery colors
to mark our turf.

We draw figure eights in sand
and bury our wordsmith designs
between the space of eights.

Anyone attached to the word
finds our ribbons just beneath earth
waiting to be heard.

When we touch the soil,
words climb vines
reaching for surface destiny.

Words whisper in the air.
Smiles lock on a moment
as attention locks in space.

The wordsmith is reborn
to massage an untouched spirit
in the light of the sacred.

Ashok K. Bhargava

Ashok Bhargava is a poet, writer, inspirational speaker and a literary consultant. He has attended poetry conferences in Italy, Turkey, India and Philippines. His latest book "Riding the Tide" about his battle with cancer has been translated and published in Arabic, Hindi, Telugu and Bengali languages. He is a contributing writer to several anthologies worldwide including World Poetry Almanac 2014. He has been published in numerous print and online magazines.

Ashok has won many accolades including Poet Ambassador to Japan, Kalidasa International award, World Poetry Lifetime Achievement award, Writers Beyond Borders Peace award and Tapsilog Leadership award for his community involvement. He is founder of Writers International Network Canada Society to discover, nourish, recognize and celebrate writers, poets and artists and to assist them to network with the community at large. He is the author of eight books of poetry and one anthology. He is Artist-in-Residence at Moberly Arts & Cultural Centre and also co-edits the literary section of The Link Newspaper.

Genesis

Just the two of us
on a beach,
sand still warm
from the afternoon sun.

We were Adam and Eve
as the evening unrolled
its orange and gold curtain
across the burning sky.

Alone—
you and I,
planting the first dreams
of a world
only we could imagine.

Just as It Is

Silence stretched for years—
hurting more than it healed.

Warped timber
can't be straightened,
but it can be beautiful
just as it is.

Roots still find the earth.

A flower never asks
if the soil remembers the storm.

It rises.

Life drifts
on the river of time—
not aimless,
but reaching
for the ocean
of becoming.

And in that vastness,
we are not lost.

We bloom.

Essence

I want
to feel, to live —
the essence of every moment.

Like rays of sunlight
breaking suddenly through heavy clouds,
I want
to kiss that pure, bright light
with my lips —
against the soft, blurred edges of the dark.

Though darkness
was here before us, and will remain after,
still,
the light is ours —
even if only for a few brief moments,
this is our chance to shine.

Caroline 'Ceri Naz' Nazareno Gabis

Caroline 'Ceri' Nazareno-Gabis

Caroline 'Ceri Naz' Nazareno-Gabis, author of Velvet Passions of Calibrated Quarks, World Poetry Canada International Director to Philippines is a multi-awarded poet, editor, journalist, educator, peace and women's advocate. She believes that learning other's language and culture is a doorway to wisdom.

Among her poetic belts include **Gabrielle Galloni Memorial Panorama International Youth Award 2022,** Panorama Youth Literary Awards 2020, 7th Prize Winner in the 19th, 20th and 21st Italian Award of Literary Festival; Writers International Network-Canada ''Amazing Poet 2015'', The Frang Bardhi Literary Prize 2014 (Albania), Poet Journalist Award 2014 (Tuzla, Istanbul, Turkey) and World Poetry Empowered Poet 2013 (Vancouver, Canada). She's a featured member of Association of Women's Rights and Development (AWID), The Poetry Posse, Galaktika Poetike, Asia Pacific Writers and Translators (APWT), Axlepino and Anacbanua. Her poetry and children's stories have been featured in different anthologies and magazines worldwide.

Links to her works:

http://panitikan.ph/2018/03/30/caroline-nazareno-gabis/

https://apwriters.org/author/ceri_naz/

http://www.aveviajera.org/nacionesunidasdelasletras/id1181.html

All That Jazz Transcends

Let's dance between rhythms,
Mirrors of syncopation,
Somewhere hush like dawning flares,
 A soul remembers when a saxophone play,
Trumpets of wisdom blend with drums,
Every stumble finds its beats,
Through a silky, velvety, silent night,
All that jazz transcends between breaths,
Feel the jumping notes of reality,
The shimmers and clangs of friendly cymbals,
Etched in the strides, a truth too tender,
Aching brass whispers a steady grace,
Like hope in smiles that never lead to hide,
Here's the map our feet desire,
Just love, just blend, just be ready
The time's own face,
No script, no titles, no ends,
Where all that jazz transcends.

Enduring Legacy for Humanity

We plant the seeds in a resilient soil,
Of hope and memory,
Each word we lend and say
Each act of kindness,
Becomes a bridge of bliss,
Not carved in stone, nor etched in fame,
In every hand that heals the wound,
The peace, the truths we teach,
A book inspired and opened wide,
A dream rekindled, the roots rewired,
To leave a mark and a shared purpose,
No monument can hold a forgiving heart,
The love that echoes far beyond our reach,
The grandest legacy—
To live the gift, the path, and the plea,
In our clear skies of humanity.

The Shape of Satisfaction

The growth is born,
As the sun rises,
When the heart believes,
It is finding peace,
The tasks are done
Praises will come,
Reaping the sweetness,
Of accomplished mission,
 It is shaping a legacy through time,
So walk your path,
To lift others to rise,
It's a satisfaction,
With the boldest prize.

Swapna Behera

Swapna Behera is a trilingual poet, translator, environmentalist, editor from India and author of seven books of different genres including one on children's literature on Environment. She is the recipient of International UGADI AWARD 2019, honoured from Gujurat Sahitya Akademi 2022, 2021 International Poesis Award of Honor as Jury, Pentasi B World Fellow Poet, Honoured Poet of India from Seychelles Government and International awards from Algeria, Morocco, Kajhakhstan, modern Arabic Literary Renaissance of Egypt, International Arts Council Argentina etc. Her stories, poems, articles are published in many International and National magazines and ezines. Her poem A NIGHT IN THE REFUGEE CAMP is translated into 67 languages. She has received over 60 National and International Awards. At present she is the Cultural Ambassador for India and South Asia of Inner Child and the life member of Odisha Environmental Society

Email
swapna.behera@gmail.com

Web Site
http://swapnabehera.in/

transcendence of the seventh note

history hibernates in the broken anthills
the kings, queens and the concubines
escape in the corridors of the palace
emotional charcoal lines sketch
names on the walls of the old inn
the dice rolls;
descending snakes or ascending ladder
grins of a looser or splattering smiles
Draupadi's mortification or Srikrushna's flute
somewhere the seventh note always transcends
the tunnel of the third eye
opens in the emancipation
the roller coaster moves fast
goes on the swim or sail
currency escapes as conspiracy
blood gets thinner than water
a new planet rotates
the straight-line twists to be a cycle tyre
logics become logistics
slumbering smiles in the footpaths
escape for a savour banquet
in the dreams
the countdown starts
for the ardent escape
the seventh note transcends
the third eye opens
liberation sings
somewhere, here or there....

a legacy on the roadmarch

when the cosmic fire descends
the umbilical cord receives the bliss
and smiles get trapped
a baby is born!
when the passions ablaze
triggers poetry and sculpture
to make episodes of euphoria
when the lusty eyes meet
two bodies entwine;
seduce the sizzling
when tears in the eyes
melt the memory
moments kaleidoscope
becomes so fiery
when body on the pyre
elements are free
the ultimate truth sustains
the fire in the seed
makes the civilisation feed
fire of the conscience
makes a demon a sage
fire of the soul
mingle or jingle
but certainly, creates the checklist of a legacy -----

satisfaction is a cushion or cuisine!

you can sit on the lap of your granny and dance
eat porridge or sip tea in the village shop
counting the stars is difficult
as painful as making the balance sheet
of loss and profit
your loss is my profit
my profit is his loss
yet, at the end of the day
everyone's smile is a profit unlimited
at life dot com
a tortoise is happy or a rabbit
in the race the spectators are busy
happiness is synonyms of satisfaction
new bride, new toy, new food, new suit
all have their own voice and choice to satisfy you
roving eyes on the rambling tracks of time
a shy girl with night jasmine on her plait
listen to the music of the Earth
satisfaction is a relative statement
time goes back or the trees run
when the train rumbles on the track
ardour affiliation
satisfaction is salt in the lemon water
or sugar in tea
certainly dew drops on the grass
are you satisfied?
who cares ….
let us have a cup of black coffee
to make our moments rosy

Albert 'Infinite' Carrasco

Albert 'Infinite' Carassco

Albert "Infinite The Poet" Carrasco is an urban poet, mentor and public speaker.

Albert believes his experience of growing up in poverty, dealing with drugs and witnessing murder over and over were lessons learnt, in order to gain knowledge to teach. Albert's harsh reality and honesty is a powerfully packed punch delivered through rhyme. Infinite grew up in the east part of the Bronx and still resides there, so he knows many young men will follow the same dark path he followed looking for change. The life of crime should never be an option to being poor but it is, very often.

Infinite poetry @lulu.com

Alcarrasco2 on YouTube

Infinite the poet on reverbnation

Infinite Poetry

www.lulu.com/us/en/shop/al-infinite-carrasco/infinite-poetry/paperback/product-21040240.html

www.innerchildpress.com/albert-carrasco

Transcendence, Legacy & Satisfaction

My life wasn't easy at all. There was a lot of hard times and during those times, good times were hard to find. I've looked and looked but came up with dead searches, it was like an attempted murder of my mind, I say attempted because to me hope could never flatline.

Why? Because I am hope to the ones before me in which life was too hard to cope. Without me, their lives would've been day after day of misery. I sacrificed myself so tomorrow could be a better day than today. The reaction to my actions was transcendence to preeminence. An empire was built for generations to come, there was no time for stagnation in the slums so I moved as swiftly as rivers run. A legacy was left for those that were close to me. The blood that leaked out of me, the sweat that beaded on my head and the tears that fell down my face had people living wealthy… in a poor place. Seeing refrigerators and cabinets go from empty to plenty made me proud, I've witnessed joy and laughter from people that rarely felt those emotions while going to sleep and waking up to shrouds of dark clouds. On the prelude to financial emancipation a lot of my friends didn't make it to feel the feeling of satisfaction for ending generational oppression.

Kimberly
Burnham

Kimberly Burnham

A brain health expert (PhD in Integrative Medicine) and award-winning poet, Kimberly Burnham lives with her wife and family in Spokane, Washington. Kim speaks extensively on peace, brain health, and *"Awakenings: Peace Dictionary, Language and the Mind, a Daily Brain Health Program."* She recently published *"Heschel and King Marching to Montgomery A Jewish Guide to Judeo-Tamarian Imagery."* Currently work includes *"Call and Response To Maya Stein an Anthology of Wild Writing"* and a how-to non-fiction book, *"Using Ekphrastic Fiction Writing and Poetry to Create Interest and Promote Artists, Writers, and Poets."*

Follow her at https://amzn.to/4fcWnRB

Happy Satisfaction

A client once said to her doctor
when he pushed back on a new referral
saying you should be happy
with the results you are getting
implying that she should stop
the alternative approaches

She said I am happy
I am just not satisfied

A great way to approach life
I try to be happy with my lot
sometimes I see where it could be better
more fulfilling
more interesting
more satisfying and so I am happy

Legacy of Peace

My 93-year-old father fell last week
cracked some ribs putting him in the hospital
cranky with pain and a touch of dementia
I think about his legacy and my own
my mother is 91
my father had three sisters who lived
into their 100s
so I might have 25 or 30 years left
a long, long time to create a legacy
to leave the world better
than I found it in 1957

Too many wars to count since then
can writing poetry
about the word for peace
create peace
inner peace for the people around me
can writing books and empowering clients
change the quality of lives
help us each make better decisions
will it be a legacy worth spending the next 25 years on

Peace as Healthcare

"Banni" means peace in Baatonum
a language of Nigeria and Benin
also means fruits used for treating wounds
or a tree whose bark is used for tanning hides
as in "Ba biin boo sɔɔ baani doke"
translated, Baani was put on the child's wound
would that we all could look for peace
in the healing of a child

"Baani" pronounced [bààní] also means health,
peace, relief, safe, and sound
as in "I swaa yari baani" arrive safe and sound
as if when we have peace
we can look around for ways to heal
and feel relief
most of all ensure that everyone is safe and sound
all in words of compassionate peace
may you find "Baani" everyday

Eliza Segiet

Eliza Segiet graduated with a Master's Degree in Philosophy at Jagiellonian University.

Received *Global Literature Guardian Award* – from Motivational Strips, World Nations Writers Union and Union Hispanomundial De Escritores (UHE) 2018.

Nominated for the Pushcart Prize 2019, 2021.

Laureate *Naji Naaman Literary Prize 2020,*

International Award Paragon of Hope (2020),

World Award 2020 *Cesar Vallejo* for Literary Excellence. Laureate of the Special Jury *Sahitto International Award* 2021, World Award *Premiul Fănuș Neagu* 2021.

Finalist *Golden Aster Book* World Literary Prize 2020, *Mili Dueli* 2022, Voci nel deserto 2022.

At the international Festival of Poetry CAMPIONATO MONDIALE DI POESIA (2021/2022) she won the title of vice-champion of the world.

Award BHARAT RATNA RABINDRANATH TAGORE INTERNATIONAL AWARD (2022).

Award - *World Poets Association* (2023).

Laureate Between words and infinity *"International Literary Award (2023).*

Beyond the Boundaries

Supernatural forces
opened the door to the brightness of the world.
She began to understand it better,
to see and hear it.

After years of mental silence,
when a poem woke her up with a start her from sleep,
she began to wonder how this had been possible.
Long-forgotten thoughts
began to revive in her,
and those that used to be dead,
came to life in her poetic verses.

When she wrote – she was
beyond the boundaries of time and space,
in a world of freedom,
of her own,
unborrowed possibilities,
inspired
 – by the will and strength to survive.

Translated by Dorota Stępińska

Abyss

It's not the end,
there's still something she'll do,
she'll achieve something. It will be beautiful.

What matters is
what she's done so far.
She hardly ever regrets the decisions
she's taken before.
She can't lament over them if
once she thought they were right.
She knows now what she did wrong.
You can't turn back time,
especially when
you're eighty years old.
It's hard to fix
past mistakes.
Back then, she thought that
she worked to live,
now she knows,
she lived to work.

By making others happy,
she lost herself,
in the abyss of toil, she did not see
that by giving – she spoilt them,
she did not encourage them to act.

Translated by Dorota Stępińska

For Herself

Nature gave her harmony.

She always directed

her endless thoughts

toward the sun, the sea, and peace.

Although

she never neglected her family,

she also knew that

 – to be there for someone,

 – you must first be there for yourself.

Translated by Dorota Stępińska

William
S.
Peters Sr.

William S. Peters, Sr.

Bill's writing career spans a period of well over 50 years. Being first Published in 1972, Bill has since went on to Author in excess of 50+ additional Volumes of Poetry, Short Stories, etc., expressing his thoughts on matters of the Heart, Spirit, Consciousness and Humanity. His primary focus is that of Love, Peace and Understanding!

Bill says . . .

I have always likened Life to that of a Garden. So, for me, Life is simply about the Seeds we Sow and Nourish. All things we "Think and Do", will "Be" Cause and eventually manifest itself to being an "Effect" within our own personal "Existences" and "Experiences" . . . whether it be Fruit, Flowers, Weeds or Barren Landscapes! Bill highly regards the Fruits of his Labor and wishes that everyone would thus go on to plant "Lovely" Seeds on "Good Ground" in their own Gardens of Life!

to connect with Bill, he is all things Inner Child

www.iaminnerchild.com

Personal Web Site

www.iamjustbill.com

Transcendence, Legacy & Satisfaction

We project,
We coddle,
We manufacture,
We mold,
We build,
We shape,
We construct,
We allow
Ourselves
To be what we become,
Which ultimately becomes
Our legacy

Some stay where they were put,
Where they were expected to be,
And some just don't
Give a damn
One way or another,
Though most are
Clueless and unaware
That transcendence
From where one stands,
Sits,
Lies
Is an option

So this is the question I pose
To be considered
By those who are of the thinking genre

Where does satisfaction factor in ?

The Suffering of Youth

We were supposed to change the world,
And we did,
Though not necessarily for the better.

We have allowed too many things,
Far too many things
To manifest without our knowing

The shadows were busy doing,
While we were doing life
Trying our best to mitigate our way
Through the strife that life
Often presents to us

We lived under the premise of
"In God We Trust"
As printed on the implements and instruments
Used to bargain away our consciousness
And our freedoms
While enslaving us to the
Procedures and processes
That kept us bound
Upon a path
In an untended garden

We cried, we begged, we prayed and we
Worked our way through it all
Only to arrive here, yes here,
Wondering WTF happened
To all those years,
Those years of naïve intent,
Dreams sent forth in to
Unchained and rooted horizons
That never seem to draw any closer

We marched,
We protested,
We voted,
We signed petitions,
We voiced our dissent,
We wrote poetry and stories
And so much fiction
Which ultimately became
Our realities

We showed up,
But we did so
In so many wrong places
Leaving minuscule traces
Of our presence
And the significance
Of what we could have become

In the meantime,
We danced
We sung,
We shook hands
And embraced.

We loved,
We raised families,
We worked,
We paid taxes to the cause
That was supposedly earmarked
For the goodness of the people . . . yet
Somewhere along the journey
We were bamboozled
By the greedy,
As they taught us to blame our plight
On the needy . . .

Well God-Damn . . .
Isn't that what it was supposed to be about?

Our nation, our world is hungry
For the food called 'righteousness'
But there is a scarcity
In the souls of many . . . so it may seem,
But yet still we pray
For redemption,
To be redeemed to those dreams
Where smiles and laughter
From here to hereafter
Are the cause of the day.

In the meantime,
Our youth are as hungry
As I, you, we once were
For a better world,
A world that embraced our humanity,
And the egoic vanity of the demons
Would just go away,
Disappear . . . for ever and ever . . .
And they tell me to vote . . .
And I obediently do so
For another promise
To be delivered,
And that is the legacy that leads us to
The Suffering of Youth . . . continually!

Her II

My dreams become sweeter
When she kisses me goodnight

I look eagerly forward
To our long days together

Each glance we share
Shakes awake my soul

Each touch of her hand
Is a heavenly caress

I am blessed by the angels
To have her beside me,
For the cherubs of love
Are her family

Her halo is made, hand crafted
By the minor Gods
With gold, diamonds, rubies and light
So I am always mesmerized
By her presence

It seems like she is the one
I have been waiting for
All of my life,
And I thank the universe
For this divine present presented to me

Some would call it luck,
Some providence
Some a blessing,
And to all of this i must agree,

But fate and destiny
Knew exactly what they were doing
And delivered her here and now
Just for me

When she calls my name
It languidly passes through her sweet lips
And awakens me each time
To a higher level of gratefulness,
So I stop to listen
To the concordant melodies
Of our symphonic heartbeats

I close my eyes,
And she is there.
In her physical absence
There she always is.

Many times
I become lost and confused
For mostly in my life
I am thinking of ....
Her II

December 2025 Featured Poets

~ * ~

Elizabeth Cassidy

Neha Bhandarkar

Sajid Hussain

Mirjana Stefanicki Antonić

i Fly

because I Can

... said the Dreamer to the world.

www.iamjustbill.com

108

Elizabeth Cassidy

Elizabeth Cassidy

Elizabeth Cassidy is an award-winning former New York artist, poet, illustrator, writer and peace lover who now resides in the Berkshires in Massachusetts with my husband and our crazy puppy Miss Mabel Sunshine since 2023.

In 2024, I heard about Wild Writing with Laurie Wagner. It is an online site where writers are free to put down their thoughts and share with the community. Out of this I found my love again for writing contemporary poetry. It is my renewed passion, and I apologize to my art practice, but I still make time to create in black and white or in color.

Things to do before they come to take us away

Things to do before they come to take us away.
Water your plants.
Give them a little food and tell them
You'll be back.
 Things to do before they come to take us away.
Clean out your underwear drawer.
Nobody will want to take you seriously
With questionable 100% cotton
 Holding onto your hips
And praying that they won't make an appearance
At the wrong time.
 Things to do before they come to take us away.
Making amends while
Mending that hem that keeps mocking you
By opening itself up to the world
Showing your fragilities.
 Things to do before they come to take us away
Forgive your nemesis who mocks you
Because you think you are entitled
To breathe clean air.
For starters.
Things to do before they come to take us away.
Pretend they are a ferocious black bear
Ready to pounce.
Make yourself appear bigger
No, don't go eat a donut. Or three.
And sing your grade school song.
That ought to clear the room out.
Things to do before they come to take us away.
And who says
They are going to take us away?

What did we say or do that is worthy
Of a jail cell?
We want peace.
We demand equality.
We feel that children should never miss a meal.
We don't want people to die because they can't pay.
Oh, yes, please lock us up
And swallow the key.
Things to do before they come to take us away.
Starting a peaceful revolution takes planning.

You Have Permission To…

You have permission to
 Envy the ones whose losses
Never amount to much growth.
Be thankful that you cry
Every time you see a cat food commercial.
Just like me.
 Just like you.
We can't adopt them all.
I am talking about cats.
Just to be clear.
 You have permission to
Carry the weight of the world
On your shoulders.
They are expansive enough
To hold the sleeping dreams
Of those not yet born.
 You have permission to
Feel like the Walking Lost
Living on this planet
That wants nothing to do with you.
But let's turn this around.
You have permission
To lead them out of their mess.
They just might be shy
And afraid to ask for clean-up in aisle 5.
 You have permission to
Covet the ones with babies
And the stretch marks
That are the opening lines
Of a love letter.
 You have permission to
Believe that things will work out.
Push back to a time

When you were in the throes
Of childhood games.
Playing make believe.
And move time back further
Into a scene where you
Played baseball with your brothers
Until the streetlights came on.
And your stomach signaled
That a bowl of pasta
Would do just right.
Right then.

I Can't Go Back to Being a Girl

I can't go back to being a girl.
Being a girl was not my strong suit
Anyway.
I mean, I am a girl, but my instruction book,
My how to excel as a girl came with blank pages.

I can't go back to being a girl.
Everyone tried to enlighten me that
I would not be worth as much as the boys.
Boys who hit baseballs into the streetlights
and did not change their underwear.
And they are the chosen ones?
Come on.

I can't go back to being a girl.
We both spoke the same language.
Rode our bicycles into the woods.
Ate ice cream until our eyes crossed.
And played "Ghost" with a flat white sheet.
Okay, you are right.
I cannot pee standing up.
I tried.

I can't go back to being a girl.
The locks have been changed.
That lone Lilac tree
Shrouded my secret girl plans in their bark
And was sacrificed
By the new neighbors.
And forgotten.
But not by me.
I memorized "This Girl's Plans" Handbook

And the scent of lilac still calms
My brain that travels and passes
The speed of light.
Can you do that, boys?
 I can't go back to being a girl.
My four-inch heels have morphed into sensible sneakers.
Do not tell Vogue.
Now I can run after whatever my soul needs to capture.
And the limitations that you thought would stick?
Have you met me?
This girl keeps moving ahead.
Correction: This woman will ask you to step aside. Now.

Neha Bhandarkar

NEHA BHANDARKAR is hailed from India. She is widely published Iconic trilingual author in Marathi, Hindi and English languages. She is published author of 16 books in 3 languages. She is also a genuine translator. Her poems have been translated into more than 15 international languages and published in many countries. She embellished with numerous national and international awards for her consummate literary skill.

She has bagged Hindi State Sahithya Academy Award twice, from Government of India.
Her articles are included in syllabus of Amravati University of India. Her poems have been broadcast on Quichotte Radio, FRANCE and Hindi Radio, CHICAGO (USA). She is a International PEACE Ambassador of Global Nation, Bangladesh and Cultural, Peace and Humanity Ambassador appointed by (IFCH) International Forum of Creativity and Humanity, Morocco country.

The Torch of Revolt

When the course of life gets lost
fill your eyes with sunshine
to make life brighter
and avoid the gloom...
Oh, friend!

When dreams scatter
and we are left on our own
then too, you hold onto
the strings of relationships
Please don't pull it
Keep it from breaking...
Oh, friend!

When the starry night
is filled with the heat of the Sun
then convert your thirst
into warmth
Keep shining...
Oh, friend!

When the mind frets and fumes
Throw off the cloak of tolerance
and don't forget to light
the torch of rebellion
keep forwarding...
Oh, friend!

Freedom is for all
Don't forget...
Oh friend!!

Keyboard of Life

Life is not a comma
Life is not a full stop
Life is not a question mark
Even life is not an exclamatory sign only

If life is addition or deletion
You must keep
Balancing it like
'Is equal to' signs
To get equal opportunities,
parity and rights

Utilise 'inverted comma'
To title your virtues
Underscore your respect
To emphasis your Importance and values
In the Constellation or
In the spectrum of hues

Don't put your life in a bracket
Put your dreams in your pocket
Hashtag your happy moments to rocket

Be aware of the repercussions of aspartame
At the rate of the maximum percentage of fame
Multiply your relations & aim
Don't add fuel to the flame
Subtract your name from the shame

Highlight your friendship
On concrete base
On the keyboard of life
Enter to make your own space

Pride

Leaving footprints on the sand
such is the imprinting of overwhelming moments
on the mind

Acquiring the bitterness of obtainable consciousness
Spilling over
sparkling beauty from eyes

Shaping dreams and
 living life in depth
awakening uncountable questions from the narrow lane

Walking in the sky
Beyond the horizon
like churning out the mangled personality

Being self-realized with the existential, serene
consciousness
spewing out of imperious pride.

Sajid

Hussain

Dr. Sajid Hussain, born on February 1, 1969, in Morgah, Rawalpindi, Pakistan, is a distinguished poet, educator, and advocate for literature. He holds memberships in global literary organizations and has received numerous accolades, including the Shahitya Pata Award and the Rabindranath Tagore Memorial Literary Honours. He has authored acclaimed works and contributed to international anthologies. A senior Chemistry teacher and Master Trainer in "Low Cost and No Cost Science Material," Dr. Hussain is also a homeopathic doctor and former principal. His poetry, often focused on humanity and nature, is widely published and translated. Dr. Hussain is a committed advocate for global understanding, cultural exchange, and social justice, using his platform to inspire positive change and foster dialogue.

1 Far Away From the Self

Our destined paths have long departed into distance,
Trails now scattered within the mirrors of mist,
Silent and desolate have lapsed these watchful eyes,
As fractured stillness veils the horizon's reach.

No thought remains, nor courtyard of old, nor kin,
We have become exiles within our native breath,
Those we sought in the ache of each heartbeat,
Their visages now wane in the fog of memory.

Yes,far away we've wandered from our very selves,
No vision remains, no image bears clarity,
Only a circling maze of dim reflection,
As though weariness clings to every breath,
And someone seeks shade within this scorching life.

Burned by the cruel majesty of solar wrath,
The valley ends where silence may cradle the weary,
Yet life has wearied in deciphering its own depths,
In quests to comprehend the soul's own reflection.

Now it seems as if none remains to call our own,
And even our shadow feels estrangement and silence,
A quiet dread arises from within the self,
For we have strayed far from our own essence.

Perhaps, there lies a destination still unknown,
Or life itself is but the name of onward wandering,
Though the pageantry of springtime leads the soul astray,
Some visions yet persist, ordained to summon lamentation.

The Temple of Solitude

By its own aspirations a tragic solitude,
Torn between pride and humility in sacred vengeance,
Cradles in the lullaby of illusion within prophetic silence,
Binds the myth of eternal return in the mist ,
To drench in devotional longing captivated by sorrow,
Dwells in the temple of thought to hush between
heartbeats,
Carved from the stone of inner silence the suspense,
Baths in the ink of quiet introspection to sigh,
A secret flame of separation rooted in the soil of,
Triumph of will crowned by the bloom of perseverance,
Crushes the weight of broken dreams with fulfilled desire,
Enthralled by loss in the shadows of imagined pain,
Casts upon the vortex of fate's austere withdrawal,
To stir the abyss of absence hollowed by the silence,
The corridors of heartache tread in the veil of grief,
With the rhythms of ecstasy to cradle new dawn.

The Deceit of the Journey

I returned empty handed from fulfillment's silent sanctuary,
Though adorned with insight, I touched not sacred truth,
With steadfast tread I climbed triumph's towering illusion,
Mistaking vain success for life's sovereign culmination.

That which I crowned as victory was inner void,
While perceived defeat revealed veiled divine ascendancy,
Through boundless spans of becoming I wandered
estranged,
Mistaking fleeting milestones for eternal resting abodes.

The final anchor lay shrouded in misted obscurity,
Yet I declared myself whole amidst spectral delusion,
Mind forged illusions clasped me in silent bondage ,
A fugitive of time, adrift through vanishing instants.

Shelters shifted, destinations dissolved without farewell,
Each threshold led toward another unnamed departure,
Fatigue etched its weight within my aching marrow,
And I sought shade beneath illusion's transient grace.

Yet the mirage multiplied, the path stretched unyielding,
And life dissolved beneath dusk's encroaching veil,
The light withdrew, the horizon cloaked in silence,
Far from the verity I once presumed to possess.

Now I yearn to return to origin's lost flame,
Perhaps the first step bore truth's hidden dwelling,
That forsaken threshold, shunned in hunger's pursuit,
May hold the essence eclipsed by wandering desire.

Mirjana Stefanicki Antonić

Mirjana Stefanicki Antonić

Mirjana Stefanicki Antonić was born in 1954 in Novi Sad, Republic of Serbia. She writes poetry, literary criticism, essays and short stories. She published sixteen independent books - eleven books of poetry, three books of literary essays and two books of literary criticism. She is represented in contemporary anthologies and also in common books of poetry, in literary magazines, art, culture and science. Her songs have been translated into several foreign languages. She is awarded for her poetic achievements. Mirjana is economist by education. She is a member of the Society of Writers of Vojvodina since 1997, and the Association of Writers of Serbia since 2019. Laureate of the 2025 Naji Naaman Literary Prize 2025, honor prize for complete works, out of competition. Lives and works in Novi Sad, Republic of Serbia.

Ember in the Rod's Box
(My hearth lasts for centuries)

Life is breathed into us by the rays of the Sun
We carry it with the fire of our hearts.
We keep the flame on the hearth of origination

Our family by the hearth
The fire ignited love.
Scattered offspring whose centuries are not counted

Who are we when the heat dies down?
When the fire goes out
When the vine withers
When love burns out

As long as the embers burn
Our family celebrates.
Tied together by invisible threads
Into the eternity of the planet Earth woven

We will transfer the embers to the rosehip bush
Duration in the hearth hidden
To crack the seeds with heat
To prolong the life of the offspring
The flame on the hearth of the Origination to preserve

Like a Sign of an Era
(Record - Sanctuary - Ours)

You will carry me where you are.

Like a sign of the era
To the Record – The Covenant Tree
I will be in the center of events.
And the old Slavic custom

You will carry me wherever you are.

We will stand in the middle of the meadow.
In the middle of the field
We will pick the leaves of sweet-smelling grass
Under oak, pear or linden
And in that tree there is
Someone's hand carved a cross.

You will carry me where you are.

On the Feast of the Heart
In the center of the farm
In Serbia...
To the Holy Tree
To the Record
Our holy places

And we will be where we are.

Under the Takovo bush
Tree record
We will raise a riot of love.

Mirjana Stefanicki Antonić

After the procession, next to the dining room
You will kiss my hair.
In front of the wooden fence, next to the stone
In the neighborhood

We will pardon the cross and the bark Record of the tree
Stunned by a blooming linden
The sweetness of the pear on the palate will be there
Because our unity is important
And we will be where we are.

Cherry in the Divine Garden of Roses

Sublime as a nymph
The most beautiful of all roses
In a dream of infinity
Proud and noble diva

The cherry tree in the divine garden has blossomed

From a fruit as red as blood
It turns into breast milk.
So that Queen Maha Maya
Can give life to the Buddha.

Is she more beautiful young and fragrant?
Or mature and noble
To inspire the poet
To protect passengers under the canopy

On the tree under the heavenly roads
A scarf of white petals flutters.
Through nightmares in the soul

I send greetings to the Goddess.
By the intoxicating flowers of welcome
Awakened to my scream of joy

The cherry tree in the divine garden has blossomed

*NOTE - According to Buddhist legend, the cherry tree
offered her fruits to Maha Maya, Buddha's mother, to be
healthy and well fed during her pregnancy.*

Mirjana Stefanicki Antonić

Remembering

our fallen soldiers of verse

Janet Perkins Caldwell

February 14, 1959 ~ September 20, 2016

Alan W. Jankowski

16 March 1961 ~ 10 March 2017

Shareef Abdur Rasheed

30 May 1945 ~ 11 February 2025

The Butterfly Effect

"IS" in effect

Inner Child Press

News

Published Books

by

Poetry Posse Members

We are so excited to share and announce a few of the current books, as well as the new and upcoming books of some of our Poetry Posse authors.

On the following pages we present to you ...

Alicja Maria Kuberska

Jackie Davis Allen

Gail Weston Shazor

hülya n. yılmaz

Nizar Sartawi

Elizabeth E. Castillo

Faleeha Hassan

Fahredin Shehu

Kimberly Burnham

Caroline 'Ceri' Nazareno

Eliza Segiet

Teresa E. Gallion

Mutawaf Shaheed

William S. Peters, Sr.

Now Available
www.innerchildpress.com

KREW ŻYCIA

The Blood of Life

Eliza Segiet

Translated by Dorota Stępińska

Now Available

www.innerchildpress.com

An Ode to Love

Love Prevails

William S. Peters, Sr.

Now Available

www.innerchildpress.com

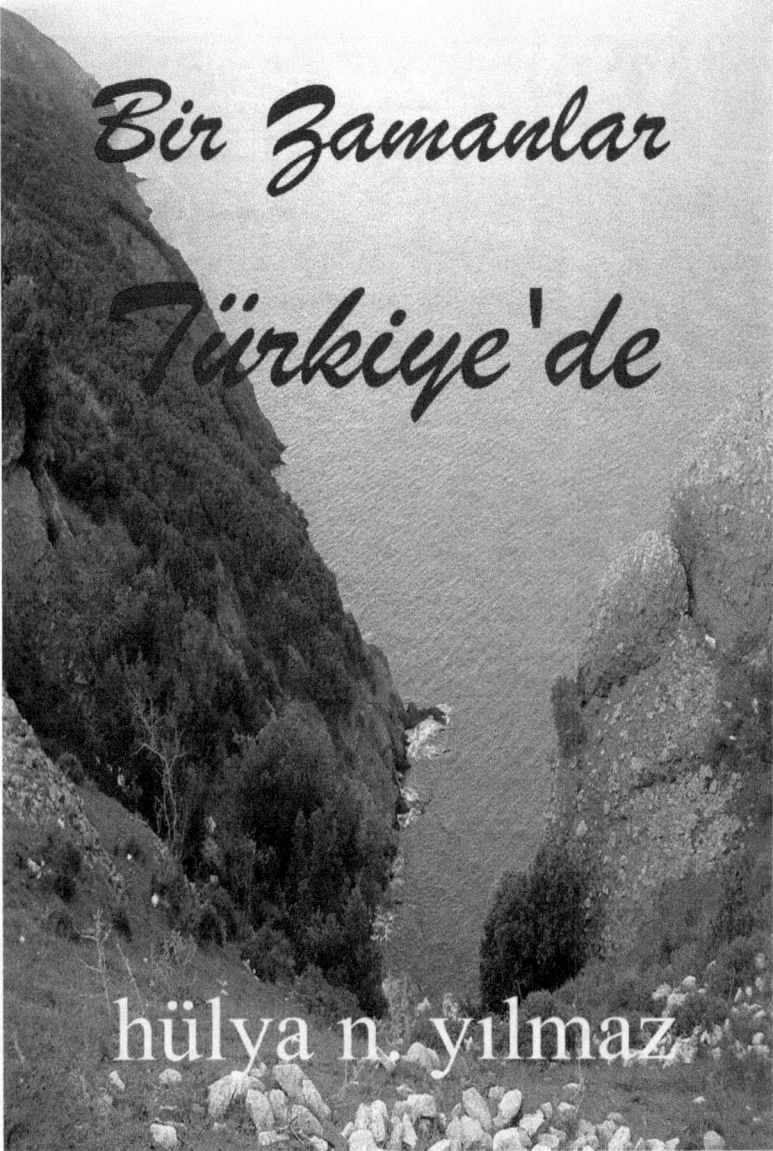

Bir Zamanlar

Türkiye'de

hülya n. yılmaz

Now Available
www.innerchildpress.com

I Am in Your Head

C. E. Shy

Now Available

www.innerchildpress.com

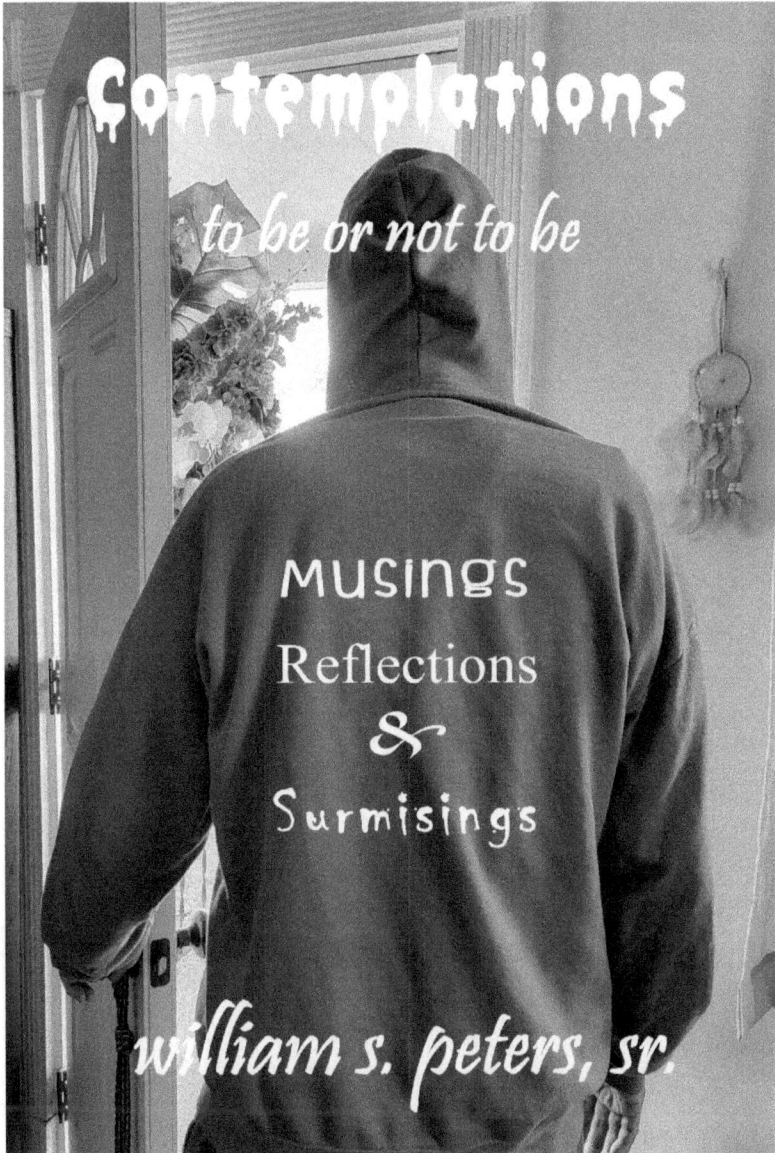

Contemplations

to be or not to be

musings

Reflections

&

Surmisings

william s. peters, sr.

Now Available

www.innerchildpress.com

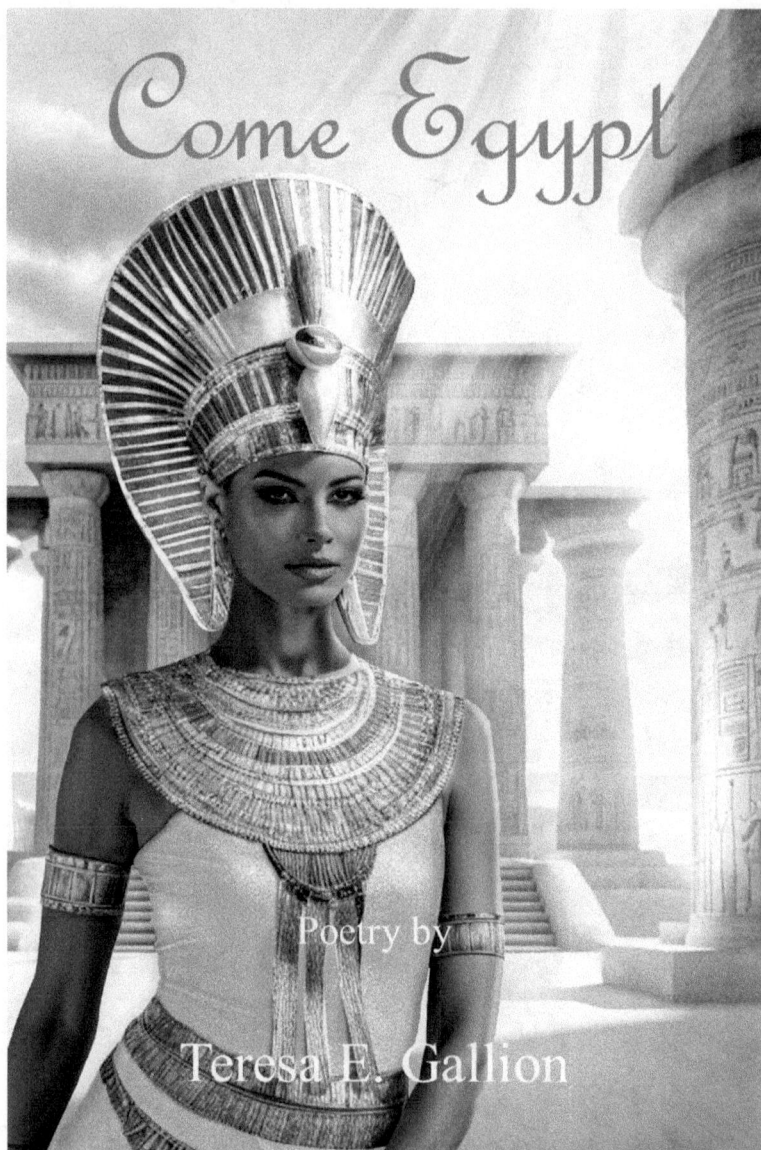

Come Egypt

Poetry by

Teresa E. Gallion

Now Available

www.innerchildpress.com

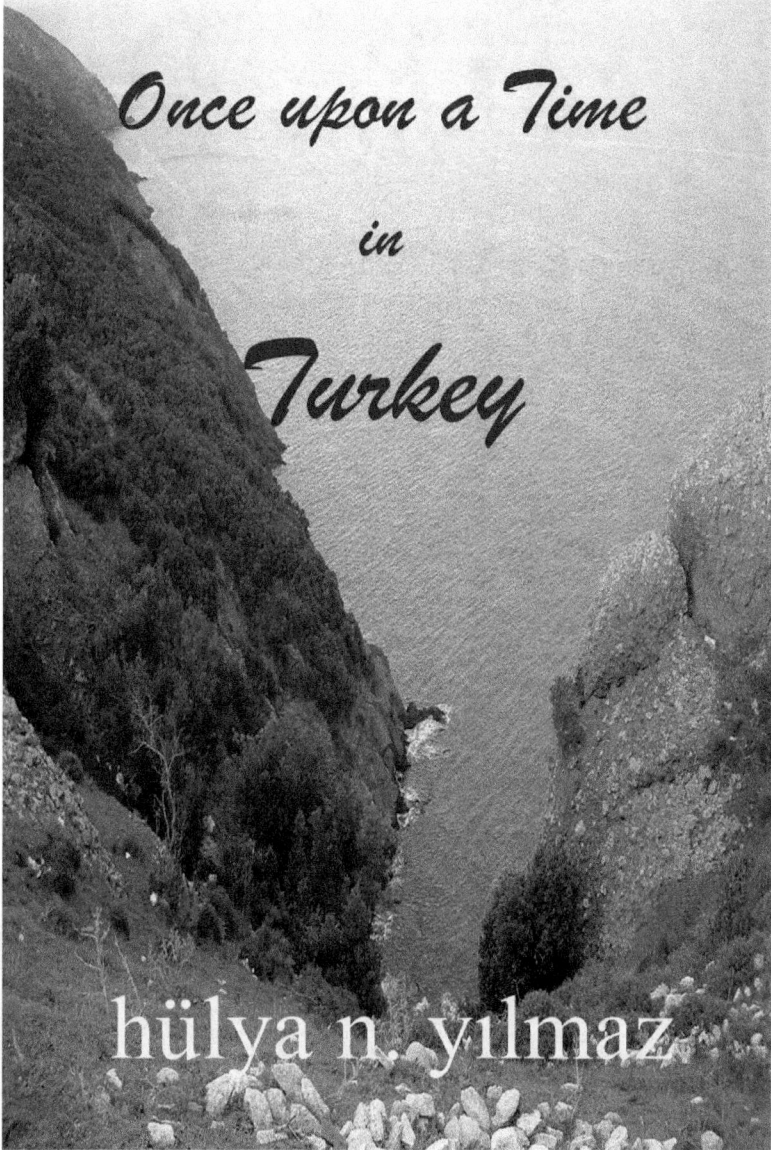

Once upon a Time

in

Turkey

hülya n. yılmaz

Now Available

www.innerchildpress.com

Unapologetically
BLACK
&
Blues

william s. peters, sr.

Now Available

www.innerchildpress.com

150

Pulling Coats

Shareef Abdur-Rasheed

Now Available

www.innerchildpress.com

UMAMI
The Essence of Deliciousness

Fahredin Shehu

Now Available
www.innerchildpress.com

Now Available

www.innerchildpress.com

Fahredin Shehu

ORMUS

Now Available

www.innerchildpress.com

Ahead of My Time

. . . from the Streets to the Stages

Albert 'Infinite' Carrasco

Now Available

www.innerchildpress.com

Eliza Segiet

To Be More

Now Available at
www.innerchildpress.com

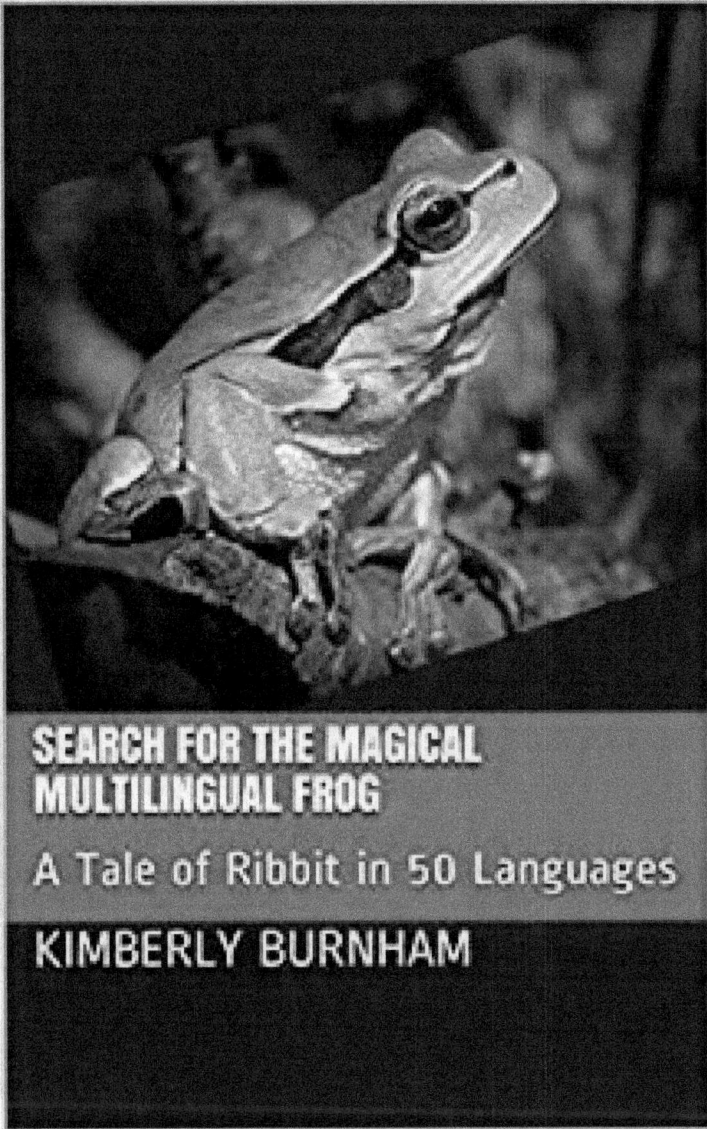

SEARCH FOR THE MAGICAL MULTILINGUAL FROG

A Tale of Ribbit in 50 Languages

KIMBERLY BURNHAM

Now Available at

www.amazon.com/gp/product/B08MYL5B7S/ref=
dbs_a_def_rwt_hsch_vapi_tkin_p1_i2

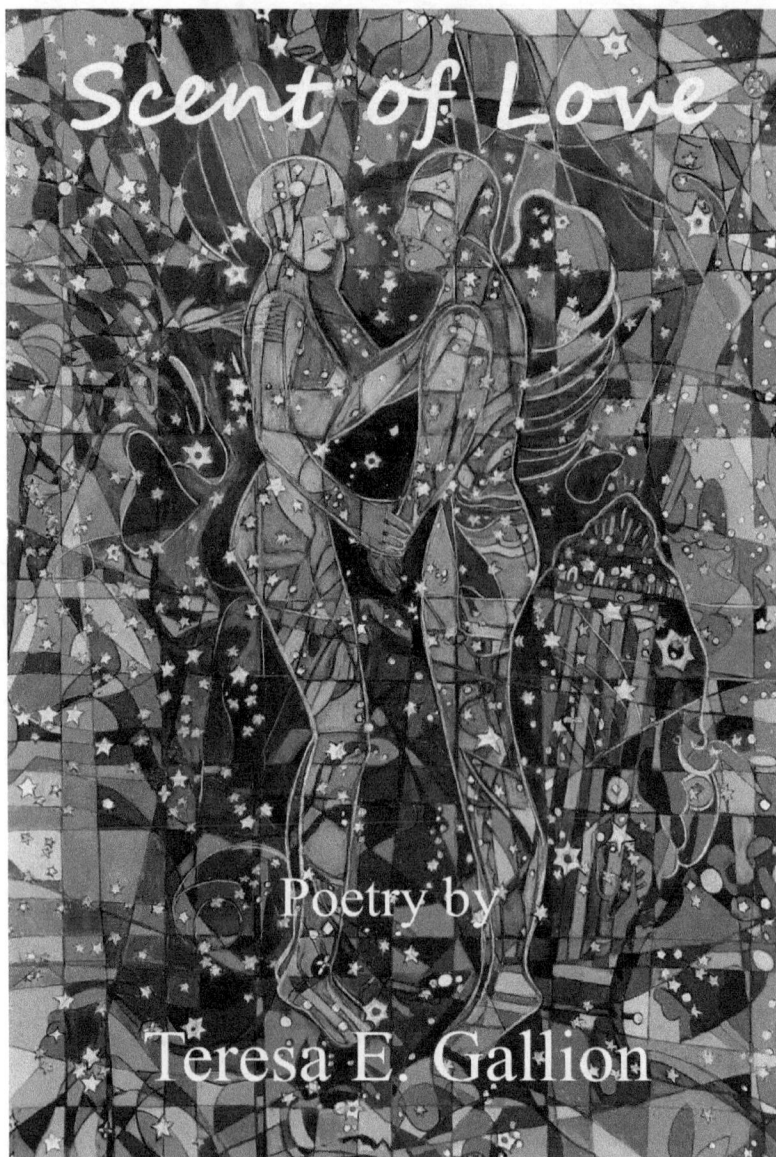

Scent of Love

Poetry by

Teresa E. Gallion

Now Available

www.innerchildpress.com

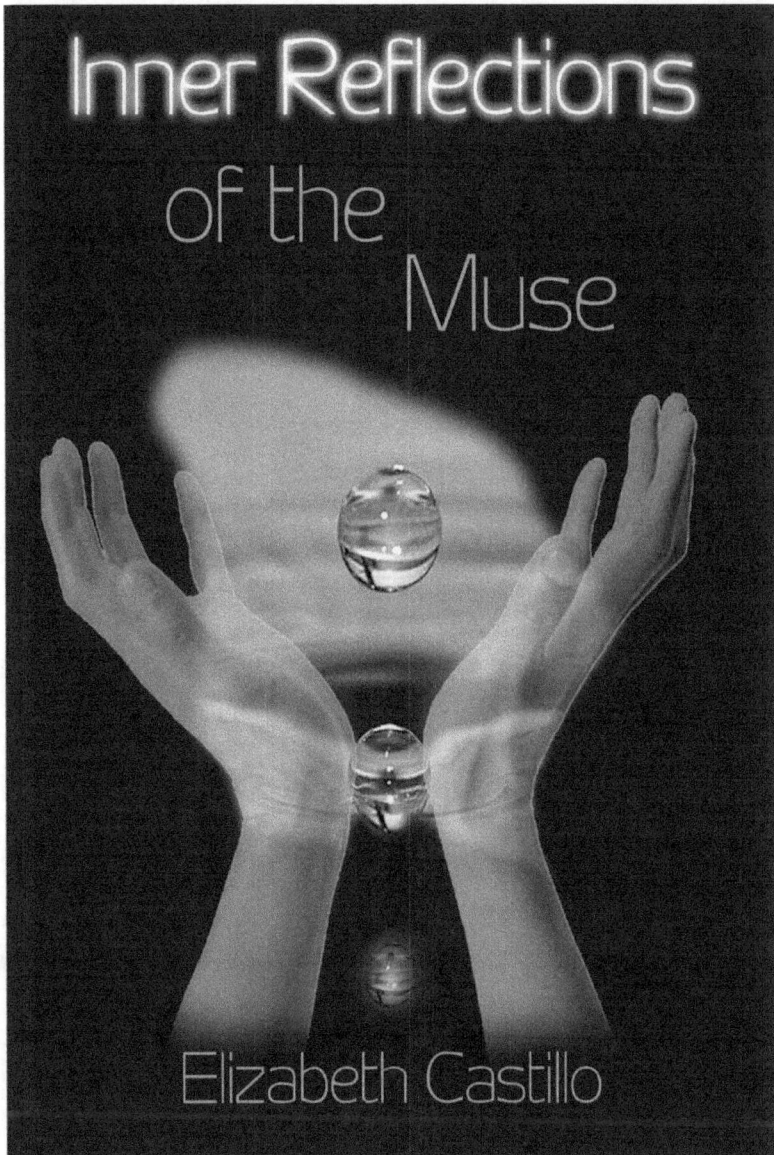

Inner Reflections
of the
Muse

Elizabeth Castillo

Now Available

www.innerchildpress.com

159

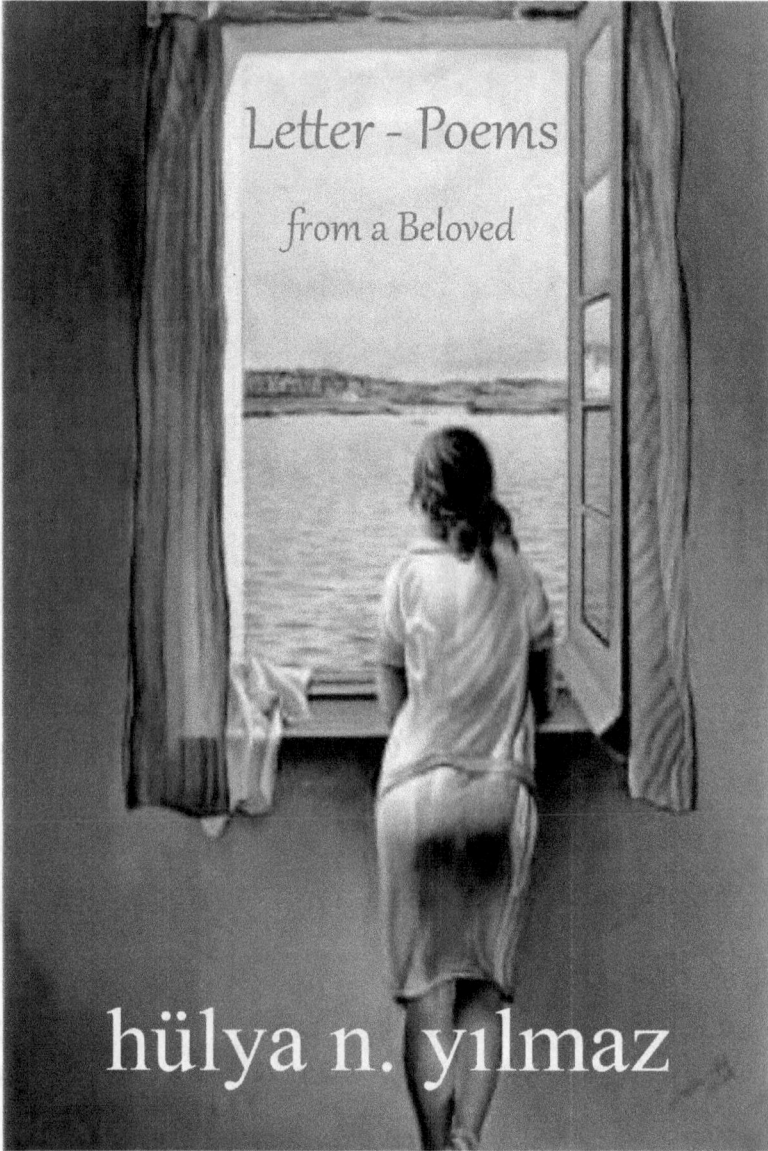

Letter - Poems

from a Beloved

hülya n. yılmaz

Now Available

www.innerchildpress.com

Now Available
www.innerchildpress.com

One Eye Open

u n i r 1.

william s. peters, sr

Now Available

www.innerchildpress.com

The Book of krisar

volume v

william s. peters, sr.

Now Available

www.innerchildpress.com

The Book of krisar

Volume I

william s. peters, sr.

The Book of krisar

Volume II

william s. peters, sr.

Now Available

www.innerchildpress.com

The Book of krisar

Volume III

william s. peters, sr.

The Book of krisar

Volume IV

william s. peters, sr.

Now Available

www.innerchildpress.com

Velvet Passions

of

Calibrated Quarks

Caroline Nazareno-Gabis

Now Available

www.innerchildpress.com

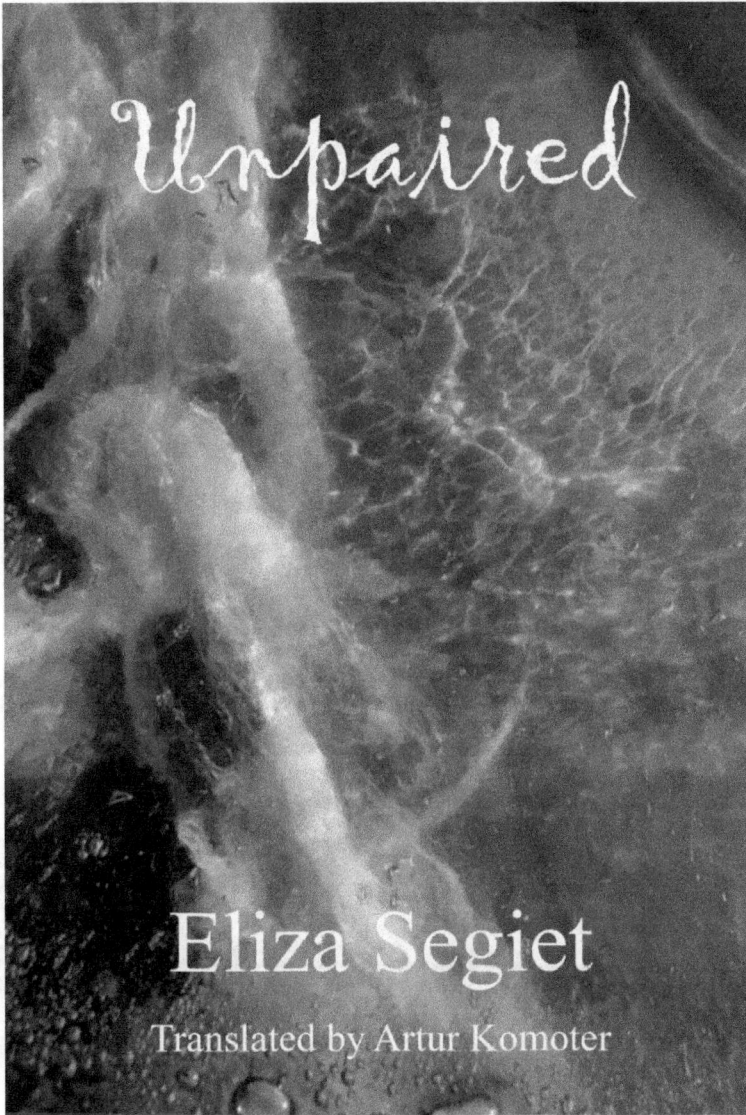

Now Available

www.innerchildpress.com

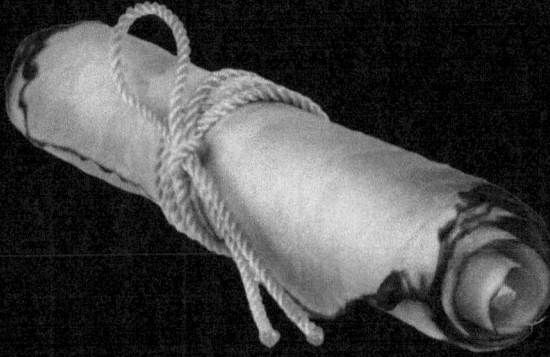

Canlarım
My Lifeblood

poetry in Turkish and English

hülya n. yılmaz

Private Issue

www.innerchildpress.com

Butterfly's Voice

Faleeha Hassan

Translated by William M. Hutchins

Now Available at

www.innerchildpress.com

No Illusions

Through the Looking Glass

Jackie Davis Allen

Now Available at
www.innerchildpress.com

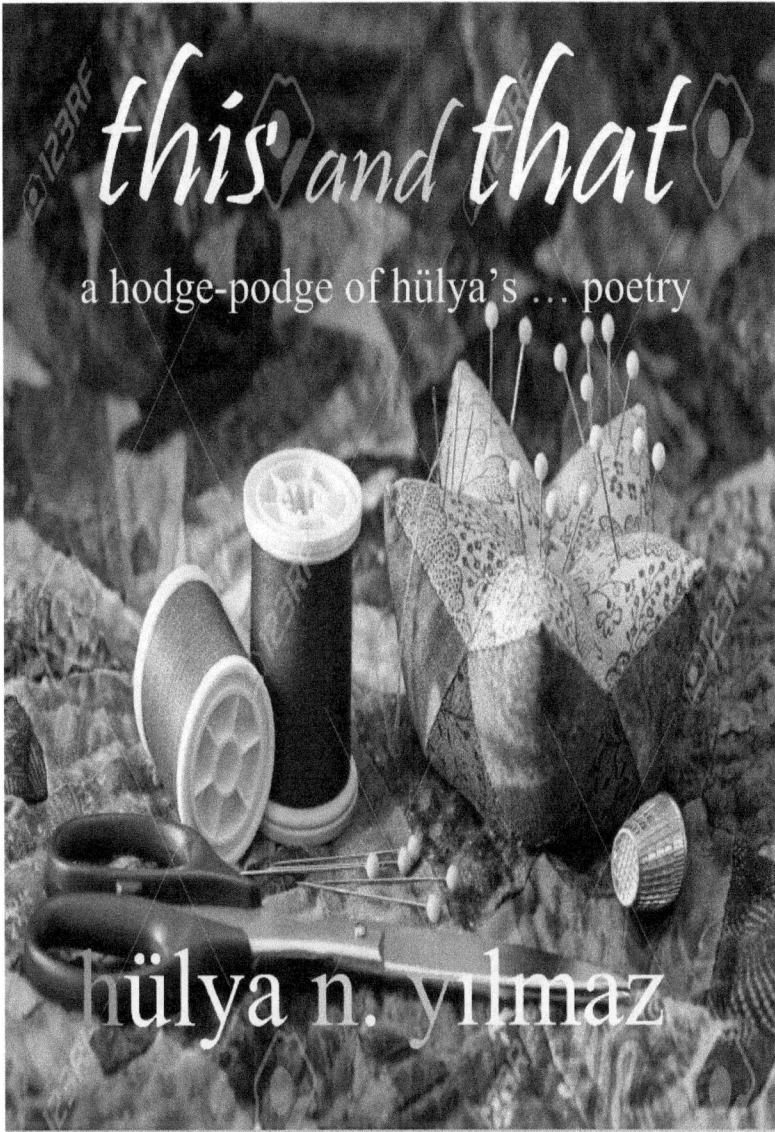

this and that

a hodge-podge of hülya's ... poetry

hülya n. yılmaz

Now Available at
www.innerchildpress.com

Now Available at

www.innerchildpress.com

HERENOW

FAHREDIN SHEHU

Now Available at
www.innerchildpress.com

Magnetic People

Eliza Segiet

Translated by Artur Komoter

Now Available at
www.innerchildpress.com

Dark Side
of the
Moon

Jackie Davis Allen

Now Available at
www.innerchildpress.com

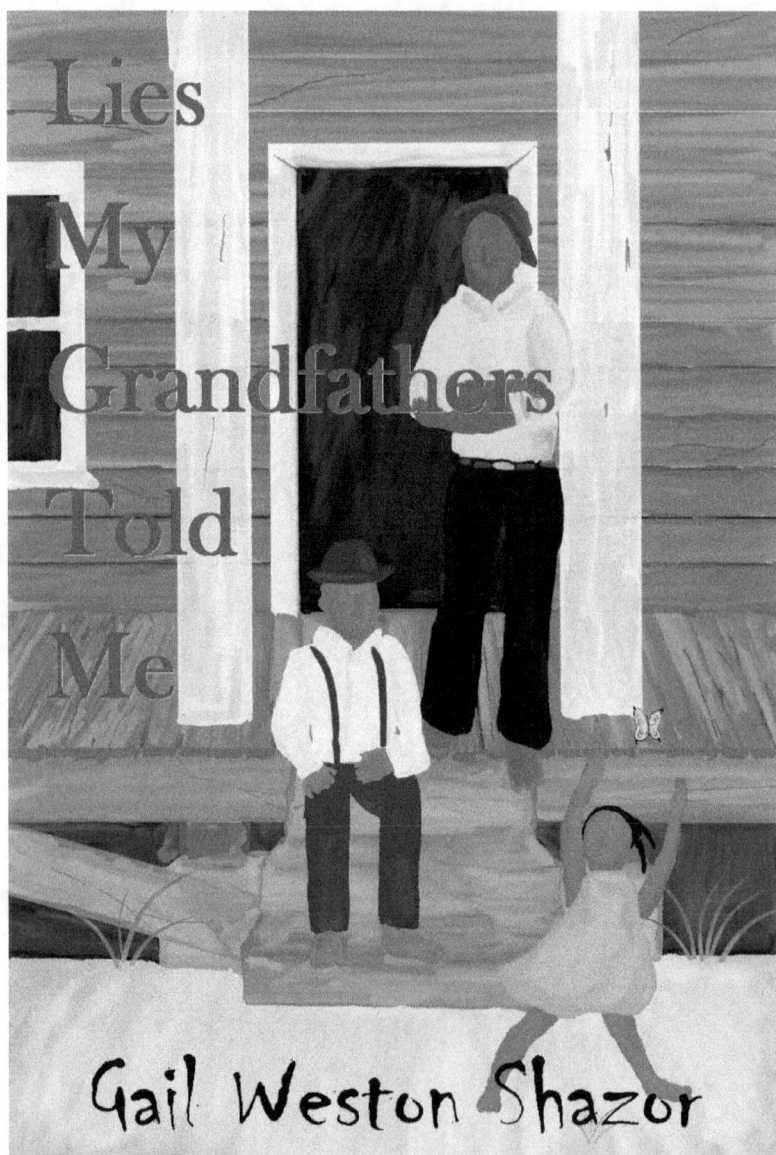

Lies
My
Grandfathers
Told
Me

Gail Weston Shazor

Now Available at
www.innerchildpress.com

Aflame

Memoirs in Verse

hülya n. yılmaz

Now Available at
www.innerchildpress.com

Mass Graves

Faleeha Hassan

Now Available at

www.innerchildpress.com

Breakfast

for

Butterflies

Faleeha Hassan

Now Available at
www.innerchildpress.com

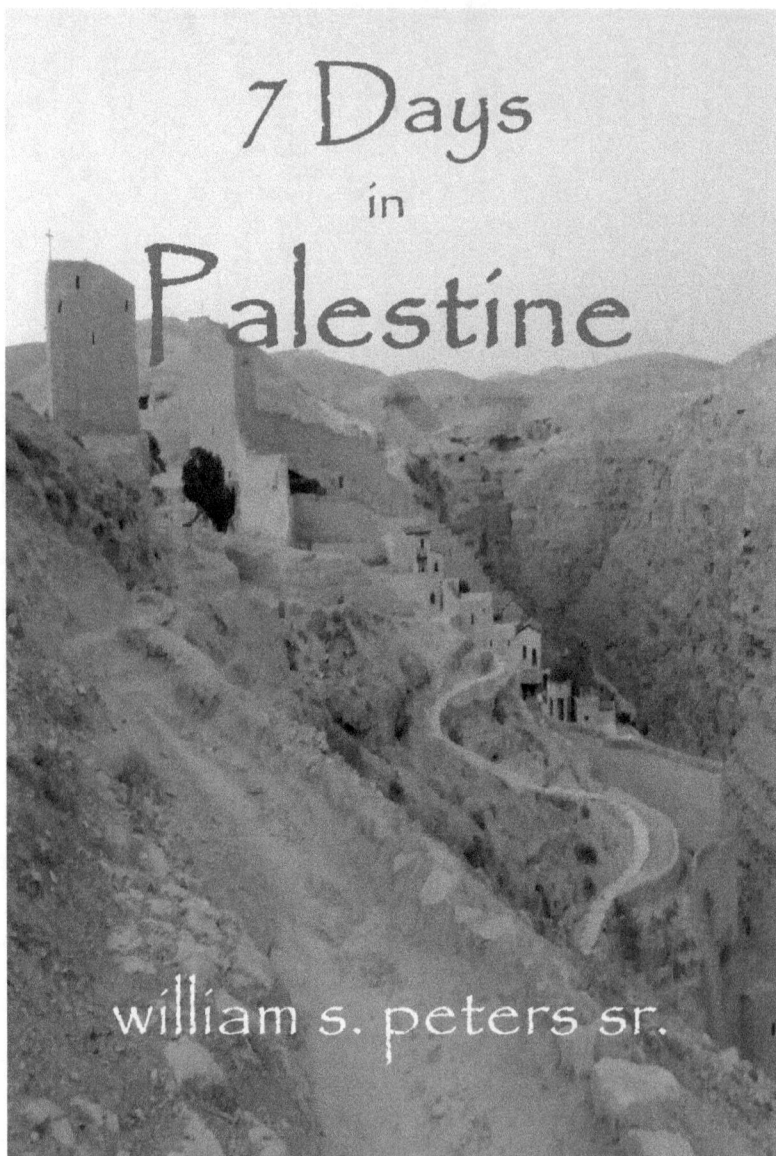

7 Days
in
Palestine

william s. peters sr.

Now Available at

www.innerchildpress.com

inner child press
presents

Tunisian Dreams

william s. peters, sr.

Now Available at
www.innerchildpress.com

INNER CHILD PRESS

THIS IS WHY I
SLEEP

william s. peters sr.

Now Available at
www.innerchildpress.com

Now Available at
www.innerchildpress.com

my inner garden

~ expressions and discoveries ~

by

William S. Peters, Sr.

Now Available

www.innerchildpress.com

Other
Anthological
works from

Inner Child Press International

www.innerchildpress.com

Shareef
a soldier for
Allah

Patriarch, Activist & Humanitarian

Friends of the Pen

Now Available

www.innerchildpress.com/anthologies

Inner Child Press International

presents

W.A.R."

We Are Revolution

Too Much Blood

Poets for Humanity

Now Available
www.innerchildpress.com

I want my poetry to... volume 4

the conscious poets

inspired by . . . Monte Smith

Now Available

www.innerchildpress.com/anthologies

Now Available

www.innerchildpress.com/anthologies

Now Available

www.worldhealingworldpeacepoetry.com

*World Healing
World Peace
2022*

Poets for Humanity

Now Available

www.innerchildpress.com/anthologies

Poets for Humanity

Now Available

www.worldhealingworldpeacepoetry.com

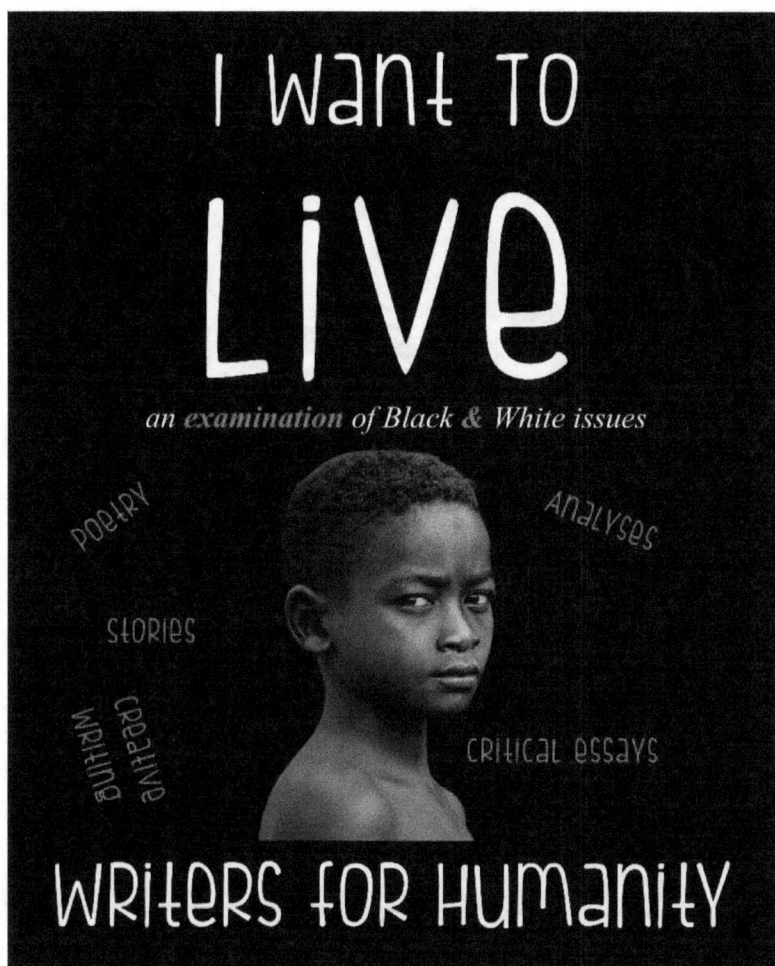

I Want to LIVE

an *examination* of Black & White issues

POETRY
ANALYSES
STORIES
CREATIVE WRITING
CRITICAL ESSAYS

WRITERS FOR HUMANITY

Now Available

www.innerchildpress.com/anthologies

Inner Child Press International
&
The Year of the Poet
present

Poetry

the best of 2020

Poets of the World

Now Available

www.innerchildpress.com/anthologies

Inner Child Press International

presents

W.A.R.

We Are Revolution

Poets for Humanity

Now Available
www.innerchildpress.com/anthologies

the Heart of a Poet

words for a better tomorrow

The Conscious Poets

Now Available

www.innerchildpress.com/anthologies

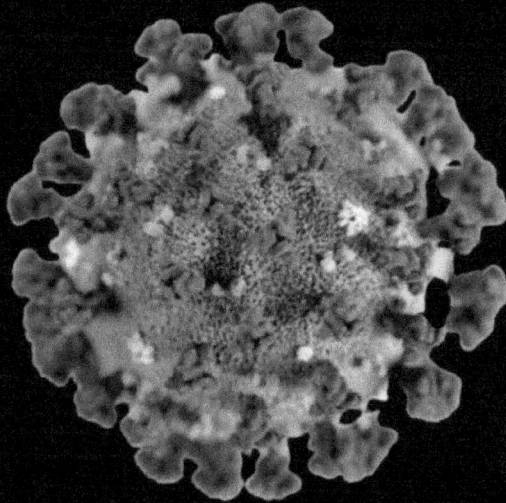

Corona

Social Distancing

Poets for Humanity

Now Available

www.innerchildpress.com/anthologies

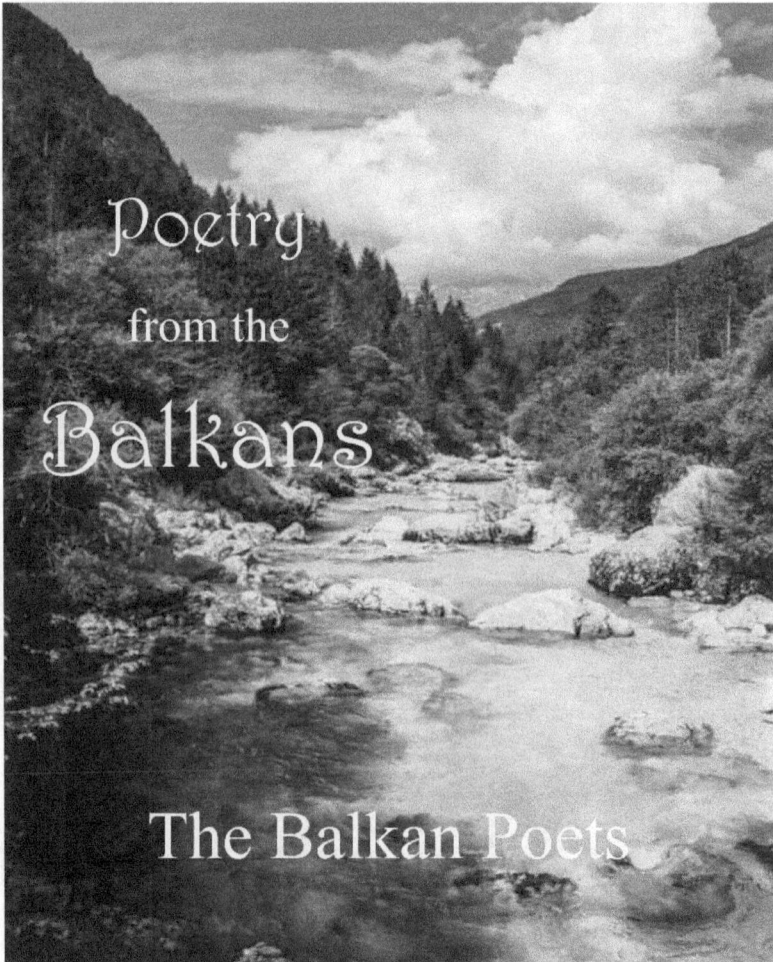

Now Available

www.innerchildpress.com/anthologies

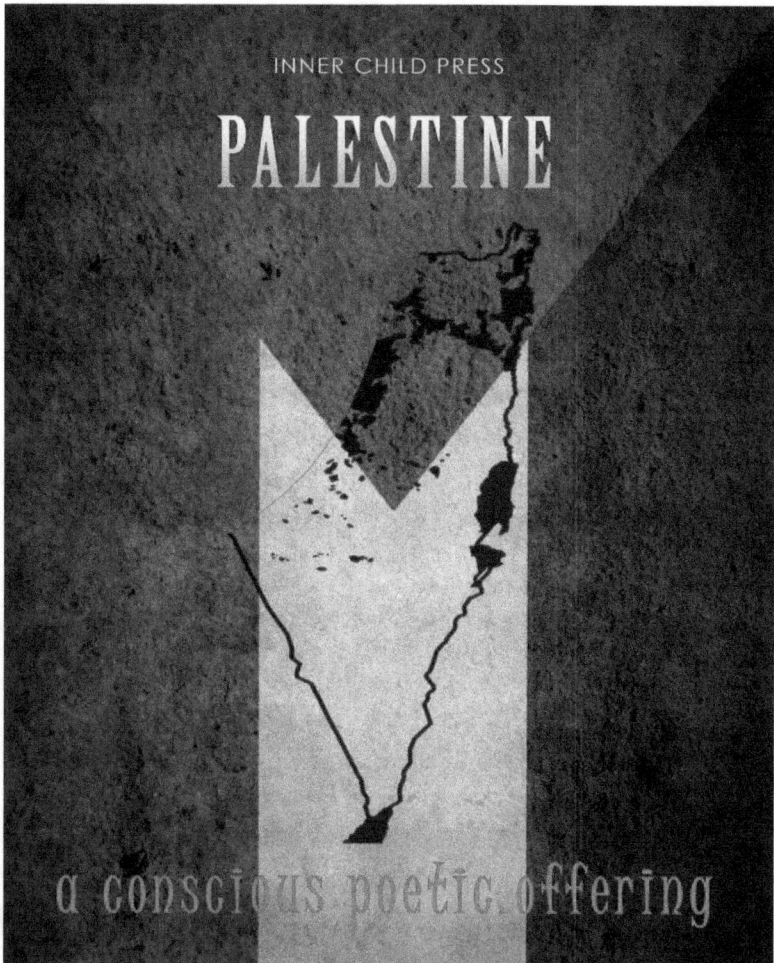

Now Available

www.innerchildpress.com/anthologies

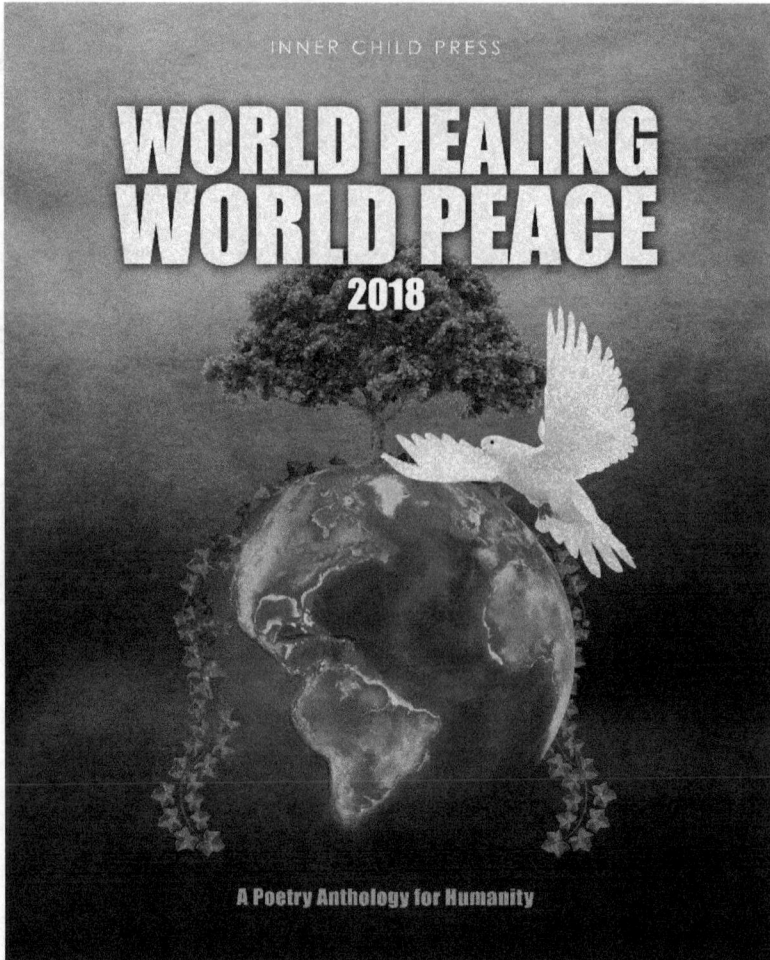

Now Available

www.innerchildpress.com/anthologies

Inner Child Press International
presents

A Love Anthology

2019

The Love Poets

Now Available
www.innerchildpress.com/anthologies

Now Available

www.worldhealingworldpeacepoetry.com

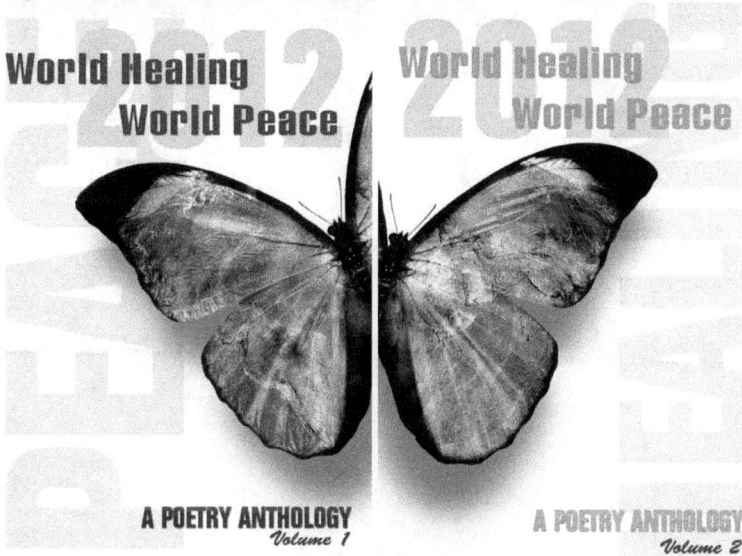

Now Available

www.worldhealingworldpeacepoetry.com

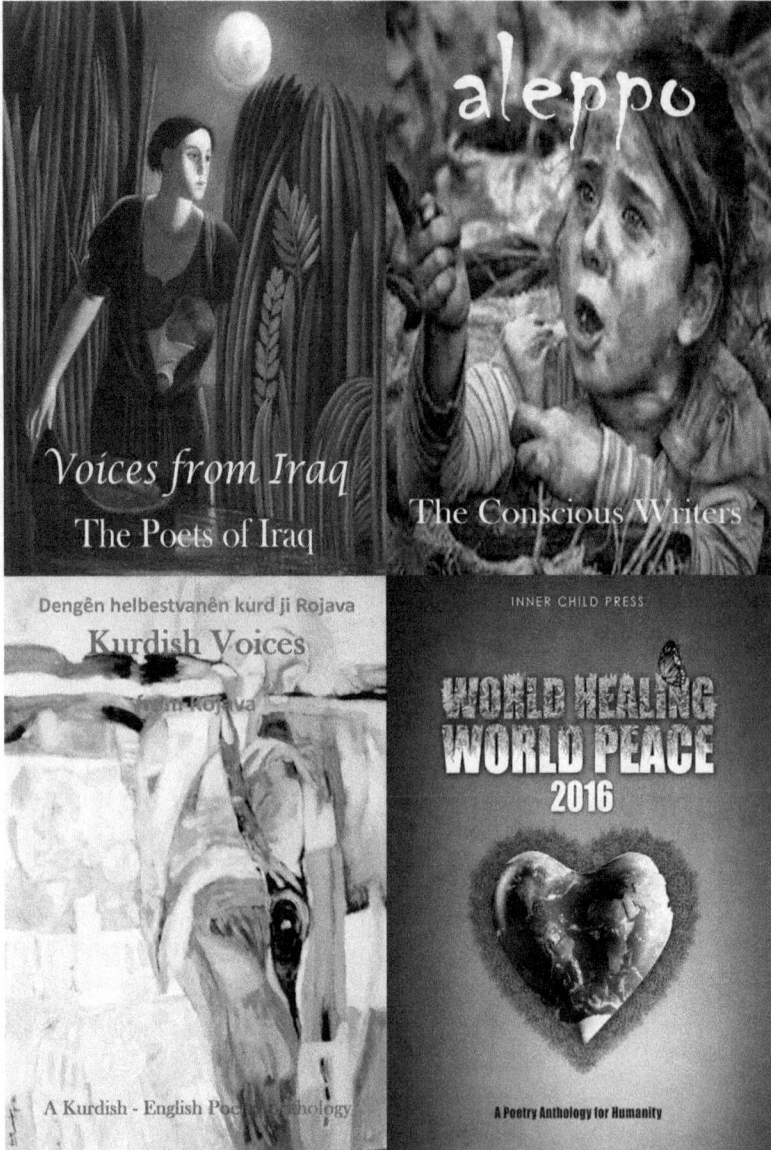

Now Available

www.innerchildpress.com/anthologies

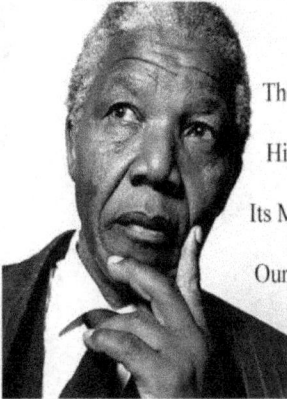

Mandela

The Man

His Life

Its Meaning

Our Words

Poetry . . . Commentary & Stories
The Anthological Writers

A GATHERING OF WORDS

POETRY & COMMENTARY
FOR
TRAYVON MARTIN

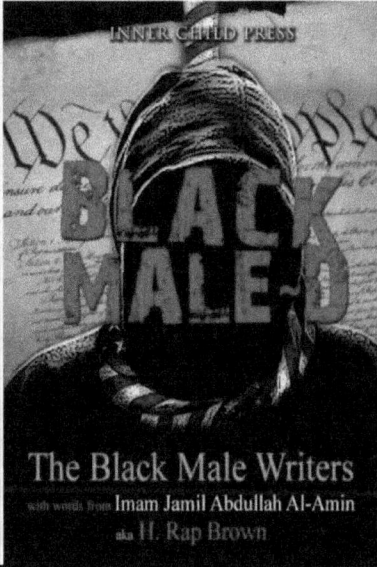

INNER CHILD PRESS

The Black Male Writers

with words from Imam Jamil Abdullah Al-Amin
aka H. Rap Brown

I
want
my
poetry
to... *volume* 4

the conscious poets
inspired by . . . Monte Smith

Now Available

www.innerchildpress.com/anthologies

Now Available

www.innerchildpress.com/anthologies

Now Available

www.innerchildpress.com/anthologies

i want my POETRY to . . .

a collection of the Voices of Many inspired by . . .

Monte Smith

a collection of the Voices of Many inspired by . . .

Monte Smith

i want my POETRY to . . .

volume II

i want my POETRY to . . . volume 3

a collection of the Voices of Many inspired by . . .

Monte Smith

11 Words

(9 lines . . .)

for those who are challenged

an anthology of Poetry inspired by . . .

Poetry Dancer

Now Available

The Year of the Poet
January 2014

The Poetry Posse

Jamie Bond
Gail Weston Shazor
Albert 'Infinite' Carrasco
Siddartha Beth Pierce
Janet P. Caldwell
June 'Bugg' Barefield
Debbie M. Allen
Tony Henninger
Joe DaVerbal Minddancer
Robert Gibbons
Neetu Wali
Shareef Abdur-Rasheed
William S. Peters, Sr.

Carnation

Our January Feature
Terri L. Johnson

the Year of the Poet
February 2014

violets

The Poetry Posse
Jamie Bond
Gail Weston Shazor
Albert 'Infinite' Carrasco
Siddartha Beth Pierce
Janet P. Caldwell
June 'Bugg' Barefield
Debbie M. Allen
Tony Henninger
Joe DaVerbal Minddancer
Robert Gibbons
Neetu Wali
Shareef Abdur-Rasheed
William S. Peters, Sr.

Our February Features
Teresa E. Gallion & Robert Gibson

the Year of the Poet
March 2014

The Poetry Posse
Jamie Bond
Gail Weston Shazor
Albert 'Infinite' Carrasco
Siddartha Beth Pierce
Janet P. Caldwell
June 'Bugg' Barefield
Debbie M. Allen
Tony Henninger
Joe DaVerbal Minddancer
Robert Gibbons
Neetu Wali
Shareef Abdur-Rasheed
Kimberly Burnham
William S. Peters, Sr.

daffodil

Our March Featured Poets
Alicia C. Cooper & hülya yılmaz

the Year of the Poet
April 2014

The Poetry Posse
Jamie Bond
Gail Weston Shazor
Albert 'Infinite' Carrasco
Siddartha Beth Pierce
Janet P. Caldwell
June 'Bugg' Barefield
Debbie M. Allen
Tony Henninger
Joe DaVerbal Minddancer
Robert Gibbons
Neetu Wali
Shareef Abdur-Rasheed
Kimberly Burnham
William S. Peters, Sr.

Our April Featured Poets
Fahredin Shehu
Martina Reisz Newberry
Justin Blackburn
Monte Smith

Sweet Pea

celebrating international poetry month

Now Available

www.innerchildpress.com/the-year-of-the-poet

the year of the poet
May 2014

May's Featured Poets
ReeCee
Joski the Poet
Shannon Stanton

Dedicated to our Children

The Poetry Posse

Lily of the Valley

the Year of the Poet
June 2014

Love & Relationship

Rose

June's Featured Poets
Shantelle McLin
Jacqueline D. E. Kennedy
Abraham N. Benjamin

The Poetry Posse

The Year of the Poet
July 2014

July Feature Poets:
Christerla A. V. Williams
Dr. John R. Strum
Kolade Olanrewaju Freedom

The Poetry Posse

Lotus
Asian Flower of the Month

The Year of the Poet
August 2014

Gladiolus

The Poetry Posse

August Feature Poets
Ann White * Rosalind Cherry * Shella Jenkins

Now Available

www.innerchildpress.com/the-year-of-the-poet

The Year of the Poet
September 2014

Aster — Morning-Glory

Wild Charm of September Birthday Flower

September Feature Poets
Florence Malone * Keith Alan Hamilton

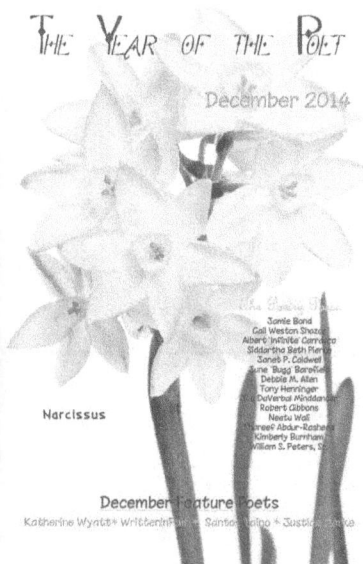

The Poetry Posse
Jamie Bond + Gail Weston Shazor * Albert 'Infinite' Carrasco * Siddartha Beth Pierce
Janet P. Caldwell * June 'Bugg' Barefield * Debbie M. Allen * Tony Henninger
Joe DaVerbal Minddancer * Robert Gibbons * Neetu Wali * Shareef Abdur-Rasheed
Kimberly Burnham * William S. Peters, Sr.

THE YEAR OF THE POET
October 2014

Red Poppy

The Poetry Posse
Jamie Bond * Gail Weston Shazor * Albert 'Infinite' Carrasco * Siddartha Beth Pierce
Janet P. Caldwell * June 'Bugg' Barefield * Debbie M. Allen * Tony Henninger
Joe DaVerbal Minddancer * Robert Gibbons * Neetu Wali * Shareef Abdur-Rasheed
Kimberly Burnham * William S. Peters, Sr.

October Feature Poets
Ceri Naz * RaJendra Padhi * Elizabeth Castillo

THE YEAR OF THE POET
November 2014

Chrysanthemum

The Poetry Posse
Jamie Bond * Gail Weston Shazor * Albert 'Infinite' Carrasco * Siddartha Beth Pierce
Janet P. Caldwell * June 'Bugg' Barefield * Debbie M. Allen * Tony Henninger
Joe DaVerbal Minddancer * Robert Gibbons * Neetu Wali * Shareef Abdur-Rasheed
Kimberly Burnham * William S. Peters, Sr.

November Feature Poets
Jocelyn Mosman * Jackie Allen * James Moore * Neville Hiatt

THE YEAR OF THE POET
December 2014

Narcissus

The Poetry Posse
Jamie Bond
Gail Weston Shazor
Albert 'Infinite' Carrasco
Siddartha Beth Pierce
Janet P. Caldwell
June 'Bugg' Barefield
Debbie M. Allen
Tony Henninger
Joe DaVerbal Minddancer
Robert Gibbons
Neetu Wali
Shareef Abdur-Rasheed
Kimberly Burnham
William S. Peters, Sr.

December Feature Poets
Katherine Wyatt * WrittenInFlesh * Santosh Bakaya * Justin Blake

Now Available
www.innerchildpress.com/the-year-of-the-poet

THE YEAR OF THE POET II

January 2015

The Poetry Posse

Jamie Bond
Gail Weston Shazor
Albert 'Infinite' Carrasco
Siddartha Beth Pierce
Janet P. Caldwell
Tony Henninger
Joe DaVerbal Minddancer
Robert Gibbons
Neetu Wali
Shareef Abdur – Rasheed
Ann White
Keith Alan Hamilton
Katherine Wyatt
Fahredin Shehu
Hülya N. Yılmaz
Teresa E. Gallion
Jackie Allen
William S. Peters, Sr.

Garnet

January Feature Poets
Bismay Mohanti * Jen Walls * Eric Judah

THE YEAR OF THE POET II

February 2015

Amethyst

THE POETRY POSSE

Jamie Bond
Gail Weston Shazor
Albert 'Infinite' Carrasco
Siddartha Beth Pierce
Janet P. Caldwell
Tony Henninger
Joe DaVerbal Minddancer
Robert Gibbons
Neetu Wali
Shareef Abdur – Rasheed
Kimberly Burnham
Ann White
Keith Alan Hamilton
Katherine Shehu
Yılmaz
E. Gallion
Jackie Allen
William S. Peters, Sr.

FEBRUARY FEATURE POETS
Iram Fatima * Bob McNeil * Kerstin Centervall

The Year of the Poet II

March 2015

Our Featured Poets
Heung Sook * Anthony Arnold * Alicia Poland

Bloodstone

The Poetry Posse 2015
Jamie Bond * Gail Weston Shazor * Albert 'Infinite' Carrasco
Siddartha Beth Pierce * Janet P. Caldwell * Tony Henninger
Joe DaVerbal Minddancer * Neetu Wali * Shareef Abdur – Rasheed
Kimberly Burnham * Ann White * Keith Alan Hamilton
Katherine Wyatt * Fahredin Shehu * Hülya N. Yılmaz
Teresa E. Gallion * Jackie Allen * William S. Peters, Sr.

The Year of the Poet II

April 2015

Celebrating International Poetry Month

Our Featured Poets
Raja Williams * Dennis Ferado * Laure Charazac

Diamonds

The Poetry Posse 2015
Jamie Bond * Gail Weston Shazor * Albert 'Infinite' Carrasco
Siddartha Beth Pierce * Janet P. Caldwell * Tony Henninger
Joe DaVerbal Minddancer * Neetu Wali * Shareef Abdur – Rasheed
Kimberly Burnham * Ann White * Keith Alan Hamilton
Katherine Wyatt * Fahredin Shehu * Hülya N. Yılmaz
Teresa E. Gallion * Jackie Allen * William S. Peters, Sr.

Now Available

www.innerchildpress.com/the-year-of-the-poet

The Year of the Poet II
May 2015

May's Featured Poets
Geri Algeri
Akin Mosi Chiúmers
Anna Jakubcza

Emeralds

The Poetry Posse 2015
Jamie Bond * Gail Weston Shazor * Albert 'Infinite' Carrasco
Siddartha Beth Pierce * Janet P. Caldwell * Tony Henninger
Joe DaVerbal Minddancer * Neetu Wali * Shareef Abdur – Rasheed
Kimberly Burnham * Ann White * Keith Alan Hamilton
Katherine Wyatt * Fahredin Shehu * Hülya N. Yılmaz
Teresa E. Gallion * Jackie Allen * William S. Peters, Sr.

The Year of the Poet II
June 2015

June's Featured Poets
Anahit Arustamyan * Yvette D. Murrell * Regina A. Walker

Pearl

The Poetry Posse 2015
Jamie Bond * Gail Weston Shazor * Albert 'Infinite' Carrasco
Siddartha Beth Pierce * Janet P. Caldwell * Tony Henninger
Joe DaVerbal Minddancer * Neetu Wali * Shareef Abdur – Rasheed
Kimberly Burnham * Ann White * Keith Alan Hamilton
Katherine Wyatt * Fahredin Shehu * Hülya N. Yılmaz
Teresa E. Gallion * Jackie Allen * William S. Peters, Sr.

The Year of the Poet II
July 2015

The Featured Poets for July 2015
Abhik Shome * Christina Neal * Robert Neal

Rubies

The Poetry Posse 2015
Jamie Bond * Gail Weston Shazor * Albert 'Infinite' Carrasco
Siddartha Beth Pierce * Janet P. Caldwell * Tony Henninger
Joe DaVerbal Minddancer * Neetu Wali * Shareef Abdur – Rasheed
Kimberly Burnham * Ann White * Keith Alan Hamilton
Katherine Wyatt * Fahredin Shehu * Hülya N. Yılmaz
Teresa E. Gallion * Jackie Allen * William S. Peters, Sr.

The Year of the Poet II
August 2015

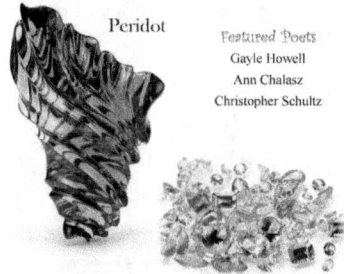

Peridot

Featured Poets
Gayle Howell
Ann Chalasz
Christopher Schultz

The Poetry Posse 2015
Jamie Bond * Gail Weston Shazor * Albert 'Infinite' Carrasco
Siddartha Beth Pierce * Janet P. Caldwell * Tony Henninger
Joe DaVerbal Minddancer * Neetu Wali * Shareef Abdur – Rasheed
Kimberly Burnham * Ann White * Keith Alan Hamilton
Katherine Wyatt * Fahredin Shehu * Hülya N. Yılmaz
Teresa E. Gallion * Jackie Allen * William S. Peters, Sr

Now Available

www.innerchildpress.com/the-year-of-the-poet

213

The Year of the Poet II

September 2015

Featured Poets

Alfreda Ghee * Lonneice Weeks Badley * Demetrios Trifiatis

Sapphires

The Poetry Posse 2015

Jamie Bond * Gail Weston Shazor * Albert 'Infinite' Carrasco
Siddartha Beth Pierce * Janet P. Caldwell * Tony Henninger
Joe DaVerbal Minddancer * Neetu Wali * Shareef Abdur – Rasheed
Kimberly Burnham * Ann White * Keith Alan Hamilton
Katherine Wyatt * Fahredin Shehu * Hülya N. Yilmaz
Teresa E. Gallion * Jackie Allen * William S. Peters, Sr.

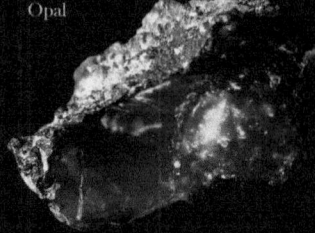

The Year of the Poet II

October 2015

Featured Poets

Monte Smith * Laura J. Wolfe * William Washington

Opal

The Poetry Posse 2015

Jamie Bond * Gail Weston Shazor * Albert 'Infinite' Carrasco
Siddartha Beth Pierce * Janet P. Caldwell * Tony Henninger
Joe DaVerbal Minddancer * Neetu Wali * Shareef Abdur – Rasheed
Kimberly Burnham * Ann White * Keith Alan Hamilton
Katherine Wyatt * Fahredin Shehu * Hülya N. Yilmaz
Teresa E. Gallion * Jackie Allen * William S. Peters, Sr.

The Year of the Poet II

November 2015

Featured Poets

Alan W. Jankowski
Bismay Mohanty
James Moore

Topaz

The Poetry Posse 2015

Jamie Bond * Gail Weston Shazor * Albert 'Infinite' Carrasco
Siddartha Beth Pierce * Janet P. Caldwell * Tony Henninger
Joe DaVerbal Minddancer * Neetu Wali * Shareef Abdur – Rasheed
Kimberly Burnham * Ann White * Keith Alan Hamilton
Katherine Wyatt * Fahredin Shehu * Hülya N. Yilmaz
Teresa E. Gallion * Jackie Allen * William S. Peters, Sr.

The Year of the Poet II

December 2015

Featured Poets

Kerione Bryan * Michelle Joan Barulich * Neville Hiatt

Turquoise

The Poetry Posse 2015

Jamie Bond * Gail Weston Shazor * Albert 'Infinite' Carrasco
Siddartha Beth Pierce * Janet P. Caldwell * Tony Henninger
Joe DaVerbal Minddancer * Neetu Wali * Shareef Abdur – Rasheed
Kimberly Burnham * Ann White * Keith Alan Hamilton
Katherine Wyatt * Fahredin Shehu * Hülya N. Yilmaz
Teresa E. Gallion * Jackie Allen * William S. Peters, Sr.

Now Available

www.innerchildpress.com/the-year-of-the-poet

The Year of the Poet III
January 2016

Featured Poets

Lana Joseph * Atom Cyrus Rush * Christena Williams

Dark-eyed Junco

The Poetry Posse 2016

Gail Weston Shazor * Anna Jakubczak Vel RatkyvIdalon * Jilto J. White
Fahredin Shehu * Hrishikesh Padhye * Janet P. Caldwell
Joe DaVerbal Minddancer * Shareef Abdur – Rasheed
Albert Carrasco * Kimberly Burnham * Keith Alan Hamilton
Hülya N. Yılmaz * Demetrios Trifiatis * Alan W. Jankowski
Teresa E. Gallion * Jackie Davis Allen * William S. Peters, Sr.

The Year of the Poet III
February 2016

Featured Poets

Anthony Arnold
Anna Chalasz
De Andre Higginbotham

Puffin

The Poetry Posse 2016

Gail Weston Shazor * Joe DaVerbal Minddancer * Alfreda Ghee
Fahredin Shehu * Hrishikesh Padhye * Janet P. Caldwell
Anna Jakubczak Vel RatkyvIdalon * Shareef Abdur – Rasheed
Albert Carrasco * Kimberly Burnham * Jilto J. White
Hülya N. Yılmaz * Demetrios Trifiatis * Alan W. Jankowski
Teresa E. Gallion * Jackie Davis Allen * William S. Peters, Sr.

The Year of the Poet
March 2016
Featured Poets

Jeton Kelmendi   Nizar Sartawi   Sami Muhanna

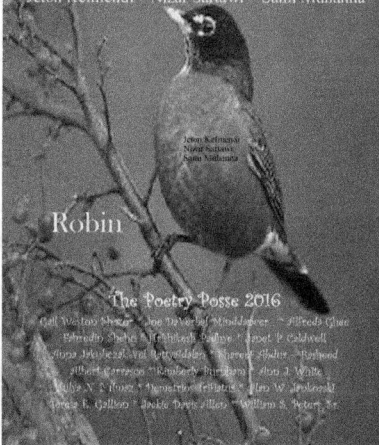

Robin

The Poetry Posse 2016

Gail Weston Shazor * Joe DaVerbal Minddancer * Alfreda Ghee
Fahredin Shehu * Hrishikesh Padhye * Janet P. Caldwell
Anna Jakubczak Vel Ratkyvidalon * Shareef Abdur – Rasheed
Albert Carrasco * Kimberly Burnham * Jilto J. White
Hülya N. Yılmaz * Demetrios Trifiatis * Alan W. Jankowski
Teresa E. Gallion * Jackie Davis Allen * William S. Peters, Sr.

The Year of the Poet III

Featured Poets

Ali Abdolrezaei

Anna Chalasz

Agim Vinca

Ceri-Naz

Black Capped Chickadee

The Poetry Posse 2016

Gail Weston Shazor * Joe DaVerbal Minddancer * Alfreda Ghee
Fahredin Shehu * Hrishikesh Padhye * Janet P. Caldwell
Anna Jakubczak Vel Ram Adalan * Shareef Abdur – Rasheed
Albert Carrasco * Ranjeeb Burnham * Jilto J. White
Hülya N. Yılmaz * Demetrios Trifiatis * Alan W. Jankowski
Teresa E. Gallion * Jackie Davis Allen * William S. Peters, Sr.

celebrating international poetry month

Now Available

www.innerchildpress.com/the-year-of-the-poet

The Year of the Poet III
May 2016

Bob Strum
Barbara Allan
D.L. Davis

Oriole

The Year of the Poet III
June 2016

Featured Poets

Qibrije Demiri- Frangu
Naime Beqiraj
Faleeha Hassan
Bedri Zyberaj

Black Necked Stilt

The Poetry Posse 2016

The Year of the Poet III
July 2016

Featured Poets

Iram Fatima 'Ashi'
Langley Shazor
Jody Doty
Emilia T. Davis

Indigo Bunting

The Poetry Posse 2016

The Year of the Poet III
August 2016

Featured Poets

Anita Dash
Irena Jovanovic
Malgorzata Gouluda

Painted Bunting

The Poetry Posse 2016

Now Available

www.innerchildpress.com/the-year-of-the-poet

The Year of the Poet III
September 2016

Featured Poets

Simone Weber
Abhijit Sen
Eunice Barbara C. Novio

Long Billed Curle

The Poetry Posse 2016

The Year of the Poet III
October 2016

Featured Poets

Lana Joseph
Usha Krishnamurthy
James Moore

Barn Owl

The Poetry Posse 2016

The Year of the Poet III
November 2016

Featured Poets

Rosemary Burns
Robin Ouzman Hislop
Lonneice Weeks-Badley

Northern Cardinal

The Poetry Posse 2016

Gail Weston Shazor * Caroline Nazareno * Jen Walls
Nizar Sartawi * Janet P. Caldwell * Alfreda Ghee
Joe DeVerhal Muddimer * Shareef Abdur – Rasheed
Albert Carrasco * Kimberly Burnham * Elizabeth Castillo
Hülya N. Yılmaz * Demetrios Trifiatis * Alan W. Jankowski
Teresa E. Gallion * Jackie Davis Allen * William S. Peters, Sr.

The Year of the Poet III
December 2016

Featured Poets

Samih Masoud
Mountassir Aziz Bien
Abdulkadir Musa

Rough Legged Hawk

The Poetry Posse 2016

Gail Weston Shazor * Caroline Nazareno
Nizar Sartawi * Janet P. Caldwell * Alfreda Ghee
Joe DeVerhal Muddimer * Shareef Abdur – Rasheed
Albert Carrasco * Kimberly Burnham * Elizabeth Castillo
Hülya N. Yılmaz * Demetrios Trifiatis * Alan W. Jankowski
Teresa E. Gallion * Jackie Davis Allen * William S. Peters, Sr.

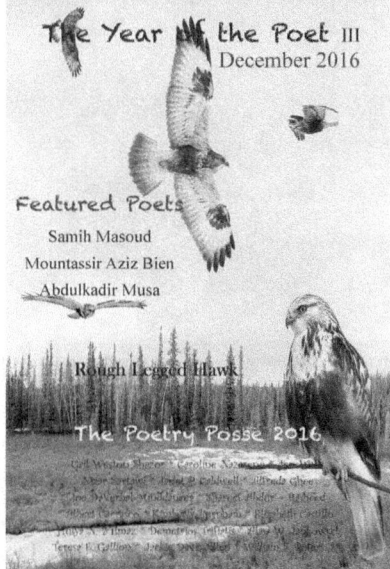

Now Available

www.innerchildpress.com/the-year-of-the-poet

The Year of the Poet IV
January 2017

Featured Poets
Jon Winell
Natalie Shields
Irani Fatima' Ashi

Quaking Aspen

The Poetry Posse 2017

Gail Weston Shazor * Caroline Nazareno * Bismay Mohanty
Nizar Sartawi * Anna Jakubczak Vel Ratty Adalan * Jen Walls
Joe DaVerbal Minddancer * Shareef Abdur – Rasheed
Albert Carrasco * Kimberly Burnham * Elizabeth Castillo
Hülya N. Yılmaz * Fahredin Hassan * Alan W. Jankowski
Teresa E. Gallion * Jackie Davis Allen * William S. Peters, Sr.

The Year of the Poet IV
February 2017

Featured Poets
Lin Ross
Soumaina Fathi
Grwer Ghani

Witch Hazel

The Poetry Posse 2017

Gail Weston Shazor * Caroline Nazareno * Bismay Mohanty
Nizar Sartawi * Anna Jakubczak Vel Ratty Adalan * Jen Walls
Joe DaVerbal Minddancer * Shareef Abdur – Rasheed
Albert Carrasco * Kimberly Burnham * Elizabeth Castillo
Hülya N. Yılmaz * Fahredin Hassan * Alan W. Jankowski
Teresa E. Gallion * Jackie Davis Allen * William S. Peters, Sr.

The Year of the Poet IV
March 2017

Featured Poets
Tremell Stevens
Francisca Ricinski
Jamil Abu Shaih

The Eastern Redbud

The Poetry Posse 2017

Gail Weston Shazor * Caroline Nazareno * Bismay Mohanty
Teresa E. Gallion * Anna Jakubczak Vel Ratty Adalan
Joe DaVerbal Minddancer * Shareef Abdur – Rasheed
Albert Carrasco * Kimberly Burnham * Elizabeth Castillo
Hülya N. Yılmaz * Fahredin Hassan * Jackie Davis Allen
Jen Walls * Nizar Sartawi * * William S. Peters, Sr.

The Year of the Poet IV
April 2017

Featured Poets
Dr. Rachida Barman
Neptune Barman
Masood Khalaf

The Blossoming Cherry

The Poetry Posse 2017

Gail Weston Shazor * Caroline Nazareno * Bismay Mohanty
Teresa E. Gallion * Anna Jakubczak Vel Ratty Adalan
Joe DaVerbal Minddancer * Shareef Abdur – Rasheed
Albert Carrasco * Kimberly Burnham * Elizabeth Castillo
Hülya N. Yılmaz * Fahredin Hassan * Jackie Davis Allen
Jen Walls * Nizar Sartawi * * William S. Peters, Sr.

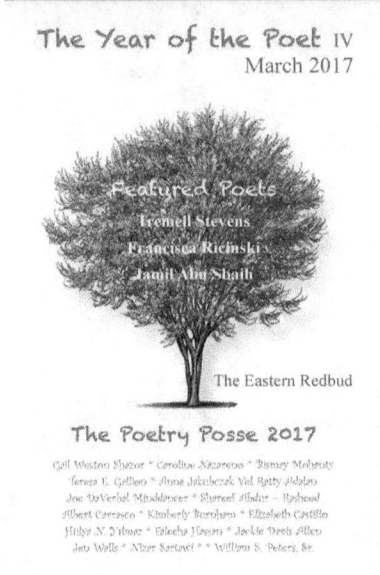

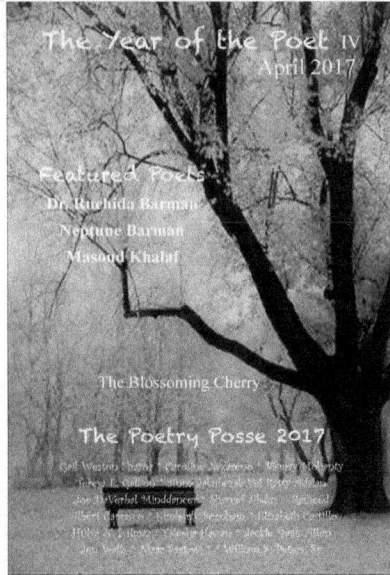

Now Available
www.innerchildpress.com/the-year-of-the-poet

The Year of the Poet IV

May 2017

The Flowering Dogwood Tree

Featured Poets

Kallisa Powell
Alicja Maria Kuberska
Fethi Sassi

The Poetry Posse 2017

Gail Weston Shazor * Caroline Nazareno * Itumay Mohvoty
Teresa E. Gallion * Anna Jakubczak Vel Ratty Adalan
Joe DeVerbal Minddancer * Shareef Abdur – Rasheed
Albert Carrasco * Kimberly Burnham * Elizabeth Castillo
Hülya N. Yılmaz * Teleshe Hassen * Jackie Davis Allen
Jen Walls * Nizar Sartawi * * William S. Peters, Sr.

The Year of the Poet IV

June 2017

Featured Poets

Eliza Segiet
Tze-Min Tsai
Abdulla Issa

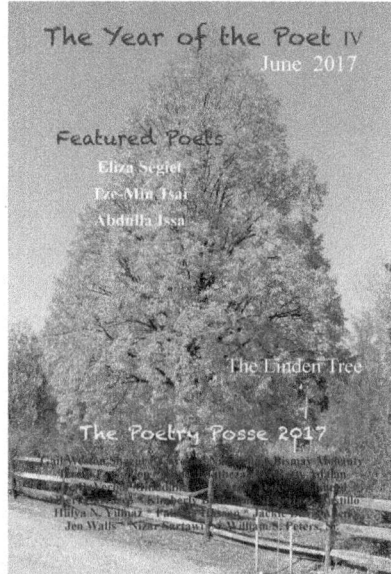

The Linden Tree

The Poetry Posse 2017

Hülya N. Yılmaz
Jen Walls * Nizar Sartawi * William S. Peters,

The Year of the Poet IV

July 2017

Featured Poets

Anca Mihaela Bruma
Ibaa Ismail
Zvonko Taneski

The Oak Moon

The Poetry Posse 2017

Gail Weston Shazor * Caroline Nazareno * Itumay Mohvoty
Teresa E. Gallion * Anna Jakubczak Vel Ratty Adalan
Joe DeVerbal Minddancer * Shareef Abdur – Rasheed
Albert Carrasco * Kimberly Burnham * Elizabeth Castillo
Hülya N. Yılmaz * Teleshe Hassen * Jackie Davis Allen
Jen Walls * Nizar Sartawi * * William S. Peters, Sr.

The Year of the Poet IV

August 2017

Featured Poets

Jonathan Aquino
Kitty Hsu
Langley Shazor

The Hazelnut Tree

The Poetry Posse 2017

Gail Weston Shazor * Caroline Nazareno *
Teresa E. Gallion * Anna Jakubczak Vel Ratty Adalan
Joe DeVerbal Minddancer * Shareef Abdur – Rasheed
Albert Carrasco * Kimberly Burnham * Elizabeth Castillo
Hülya N. Yılmaz * Teleshe Hassen * Jackie Davis Allen
Jen Walls * Nizar Sartawi * * William S. Peters, Sr.

Now Available

www.innerchildpress.com/the-year-of-the-poet

The Year of the Poet IV
September 2017

Featured Poets

Martina Reisz Newberry
Ameer Nassir
Christine Fulco Neal
Robert Neal

The Elm Tree

The Poetry Posse 2017

Gail Weston Shazor * Caroline Nazareno * Bismay Mohanty
Teresa E. Gallion * Anna Jakubczak Vel Ratty Adalan
Joe DaVerbal Minddancer * Shareef Abdur – Rasheed
Albert Carrasco * Kimberly Burnham * Elizabeth Castillo
Hülya N. Yılmaz * Faleeha Hassan * Jackie Davis Allen
Jen Walls * Nizar Sartawi * * William S. Peters, Sr.

The Year of the Poet IV
October 2017

Featured Poets

Ahmed Abu Saleem
Nedal Al-Qaeim
Sadeddin Shahin

The Black Walnut Tree

The Poetry Posse 2017

Gail Weston Shazor * Caroline Nazareno * Bismay Mohanty
Teresa E. Gallion * Anna Jakubczak Vel Ratty Adalan
Joe DaVerbal Minddancer * Shareef Abdur – Rasheed
Albert Carrasco * Kimberly Burnham * Elizabeth Castillo
Hülya N. Yılmaz * Faleeha Hassan * Jackie Davis Allen
Jen Walls * Nizar Sartawi * * William S. Peters, Sr.

The Year of the Poet IV
November 2017

Featured Poets

Kay Peters
Alfreda D. Ghee
Gabriella Garofalo
Rosemary Cappello

The Tree of Life

The Poetry Posse 2017

Gail Weston Shazor * Caroline Nazareno * Bismay Mohanty
Teresa E. Gallion * Anna Jakubczak Vel Ratty Adalan
Joe DaVerbal Minddancer * Shareef Abdur – Rasheed
Albert Carrasco * Kimberly Burnham * Elizabeth Castillo
Hülya N. Yılmaz * Faleeha Hassan * Jackie Davis Allen
Jen Walls * Nizar Sartawi * William S. Peters, Sr.

The Year of the Poet IV
December 2017

Featured Poets

Justice Clarke
Mariel M. Pabroa
Kiley Brown

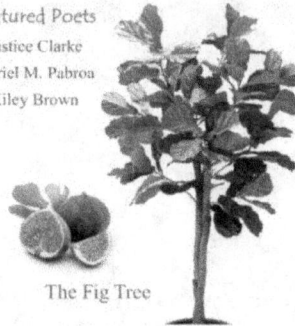

The Fig Tree

The Poetry Posse 2017

Gail Weston Shazor * Caroline Nazareno * Bismay Mohanty
Teresa E. Gallion * Anna Jakubczak Vel Ratty Adalan
Joe DaVerbal Minddancer * Shareef Abdur – Rasheed
Albert Carrasco * Kimberly Burnham * Elizabeth Castillo
Hülya N. Yılmaz * Faleeha Hassan * Jackie Davis Allen
Jen Walls * Nizar Sartawi * William S. Peters, Sr.

Now Available

www.innerchildpress.com/the-year-of-the-poet

The Year of the Poet V
January 2018

Featured Poets

Iyad Shamasnah

Yasmeen Hamzeh

Ali Abdolrezaei

Aksum

The Poetry Posse 2018

Gail Weston Shazor * Caroline Nazareno * Tezmin Ition Tsai
Hülya N. Yılmaz * Faleeha Hassan * Jackie Davis Allen
Teresa E. Gallion * Anna Jakubczak Vel Ratty Adalan
Alicja Maria Kubełska * Shareef Abdur – Rasheed
Kimberly Burnham * Elizabeth Castillo
Nizar Sartawi * William S. Peters, Sr.

The Year of the Poet V
February 2018

Sabean

Featured Poets

Muhammad Azram

Anna Szawracka

Abhilipsa Kuanar

Aanika Aery

The Poetry Posse 2018

Gail Weston Shazor * Caroline Nazareno * Tezmin Ition Tsai
Hülya N. Yılmaz * Faleeha Hassan * Jackie Davis Allen
Teresa E. Gallion * Anna Jakubczak Vel Ratty Adalan
Alicja Maria Kubełska * Shareef Abdur – Rasheed
Kimberly Burnham * Elizabeth Castillo
Nizar Sartawi * William S. Peters, Sr.

The Year of the Poet V
March 2018

Featured Poets

Iram Fatima 'Ashi'
Cassandra Swan
Jaleel Khazaal
Shazia Zaman

Caribbean
&
Middle America

The Poetry Posse 2018

Gail Weston Shazor * Nizar Sartawi * Hülya N. Yılmaz
Jackie Davis Allen * Caroline 'Ceri' Nazareno
Alicja Maria Kubełska * Teresa E. Gallion
Faleeha Hassan * Shareef Abdur – Rasheed
Kimberly Burnham * Elizabeth Castillo
Tezmin Ition Tsai * William S. Peters, Sr.

The Year of the Poet V
April 2018

Featured Poets

The Nez Perce

The Poetry Posse 2018

Now Available

www.innerchildpress.com/the-year-of-the-poet

The Year of the Poet V
May 2018

Featured Poets

Zaidy Carveon de Lipot Jr
Sylwia K. Malinowska
Lindita Ahmeti
Ofilia Pordan

The Sumerians

The Poetry Posse 2018

Gail Weston Shazor * Nizar Sartawi * Hülya N. Yılmaz
Jackie Davis Allen * Caroline 'Ceri' Nazareno
Alicja Maria Kuberska * Teresa E. Gallion
Kimberly Burnham * Shareef Abdur – Rasheed
Faleeha Hassan * Elizabeth Castillo * Swapna Behera
Tezmin Ition Tsai * William S. Peters, Sr.

The Year of the Poet V
June 2018

Featured Poets

Bilall Maliqi * Daim Miftari * Gojko Božović * Sofija Živković

The Paleo Indians

The Poetry Posse 2018

Gail Weston Shazor * Nizar Sartawi * Hülya N. Yılmaz
Jackie Davis Allen * Caroline 'Ceri' Nazareno
Alicja Maria Kuberska * Teresa E. Gallion
Kimberly Burnham * Shareef Abdur – Rasheed
Faleeha Hassan * Elizabeth Castillo * Swapna Behera
Tezmin Ition Tsai * William S. Peters, Sr.

The Year of the Poet V
July 2018

Featured Poets

Padmaja Iyengar-Paddy
Mohammad Ikbal Haque
Eliza Segiet
Tom Higgins

Oceania

The Poetry Posse 2018

Gail Weston Shazor * Nizar Sartawi * Hülya N. Yılmaz
Jackie Davis Allen * Caroline 'Ceri' Nazareno
Alicja Maria Kuberska * Teresa E. Gallion
Kimberly Burnham * Shareef Abdur – Rasheed
Faleeha Hassan * Elizabeth Castillo * Swapna Behera
Tezmin Ition Tsai * William S. Peters, Sr.

The Year of the Poet V
August 2018

Featured Poets

Hussein Habasch * Mircea Dan Duta * Naida Mujkić * Swagat Das

The Lapita

The Poetry Posse 2018

Gail Weston Shazor * Nizar Sartawi * Hülya N. Yılmaz
Jackie Davis Allen * Caroline 'Ceri' Nazareno
Alicja Maria Kuberska * Teresa E. Gallion
Kimberly Burnham * Shareef Abdur – Rasheed
Ashok K. Bhargava* Elizabeth Castillo * Swapna Behaera
Tezmin Ition Tsai * William S. Peters, Sr.

Now Available
www.innerchildpress.com/the-year-of-the-poet

The Year of the Poet V
September 2018

The Aztecs & Incas

Featured Poets
Kolade Olanrewaju Freedom
Eliza Segiet
Mother Hussaini Abdul Ghani
Lily Swarn

The Poetry Posse 2018

Gail Weston Shazor * Nizar Sartawi * Hülya N. Yılmaz
Jackie Davis Allen * Caroline 'Ceri' Nazareno
Alicja Maria Kuberska * Teresa E. Gallion
Kimberly Burnham * Shareef Abdur – Rasheed
Ashok K. Bhargava * Elizabeth Castillo * Swapna Behera
Tezmin Ition Tsai * William S. Peters, Sr.

The Year of the Poet V
October 2018

Featured Poets
Alicia Minjarez * Lonnice Weeks-Badley
Lopamudra Mishra * Abdelwahed Souayah

Bengali

The Poetry Posse 2018

Gail Weston Shazor * Nizar Sartawi * Hülya N. Yılmaz
Jackie Davis Allen * Caroline 'Ceri' Nazareno
Alicja Maria Kuberska * Teresa E. Gallion
Kimberly Burnham * Shareef Abdur – Rasheed
Ashok K. Bhargava * Elizabeth Castillo * Swapna Behera
Tezmin Ition Tsai * William S. Peters, Sr.

The Year of the Poet V
November 2018

Featured Poets
Michelle Joan Barulich * Monsif Beroual
Krystyna Konecka * Nassira Nezzar

The Poetry Posse 2018

Gail Weston Shazor * Nizar Sartawi * Hülya N. Yılmaz
Jackie Davis Allen * Caroline 'Ceri' Nazareno
Alicja Maria Kuberska * Teresa E. Gallion
Kimberly Burnham * Shareef Abdur – Rasheed
Ashok K. Bhargava * Elizabeth Castillo * Swapna Behera
Tezmin Ition Tsai * William S. Peters, Sr.

The Year of the Poet V
December 2018

Featured Poets
Rose Terranova Cirigliano
Joanna Kalinowska
Sokolović Emin
Dr. T. Ashok Chakravarthy

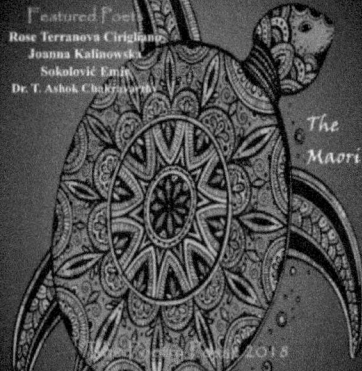

The Maori

The Poetry Posse 2018

Gail Weston Shazor * Nizar Sartawi * Hülya N. Yılmaz
Jackie Davis Allen * Caroline 'Ceri' Nazareno
Alicja Maria Kuberska * Teresa E. Gallion
Kimberly Burnham * Shareef Abdur – Rasheed
Ashok K. Bhargava * Elizabeth Castillo * Swapna Behera
Tezmin Ition Tsai * William S. Peters, Sr.

Now Available

www.innerchildpress.com/the-year-of-the-poet

223

The Year of the Poet VI
January 2019

Indigenous North Americans

Featured Poets

Houda Elfchtali
Anthony Briscoe
Iram Fatima 'Ashi'
Dr. K. K. Mathew

Dream Catcher

The Poetry Posse 2019

Gail Weston Shazor * Joe Paire * Hülya N. Yılmaz
Jackie Davis Allen * Caroline 'Ceri' Nazareno
Alicja Maria Kuberska * Teresa E. Gallion
Kimberly Burnham * Shareef Abdur – Rasheed
Ashok K. Bhargava * Elizabeth Castillo * Swapna Behera
Tezmin Ition Tsai * William S. Peters, Sr.

The Year of the Poet VI
February 2019

Featured Poets
Marek Łukaszewicz * Bharati Nayak
Aida G. Roque * Jean-Jacques Fournier

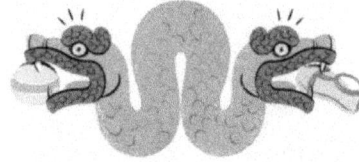

Meso-America

The Poetry Posse 2019

Gail Weston Shazor * Albert Carrasco * Hülya N. Yılmaz
Jackie Davis Allen * Caroline Nazareno * Eliza Segiet
Alicja Maria Kuberska * Teresa E. Gallion * Joe Paire
Kimberly Burnham * Shareef Abdur – Rasheed
Ashok K. Bhargava * Elizabeth Castillo * Swapna Behera
Tezmin Ition Tsai * William S. Peters, Sr.

The Year of the Poet VI
March 2019

Featured Poets
Eriosa Mahmud * Sylwia K. Malinowska
Shurouk Hammoud * Anwer Ghani

The Caribbean

The Poetry Posse 2019

Gail Weston Shazor * Albert Carrasco * Hülya N. Yılmaz
Jackie Davis Allen * Caroline Nazareno * Eliza Segiet
Alicja Maria Kuberska * Teresa E. Gallion * Joe Paire
Kimberly Burnham * Shareef Abdur – Rasheed
Ashok K. Bhargava * Elizabeth Castillo * Swapna Behera
Tezmin Ition Tsai * William S. Peters, Sr.

The Year of the Poet VI
April 2019

Featured Poets
DL Davis * Michelle Joan Barulich
Lulëzim Haziri * Faleeha Hassan

Central & West Africa

The Poetry Posse 2019

Gail Weston Shazor * Albert Carrasco * Hülya N. Yılmaz
Jackie Davis Allen * Caroline Nazareno * Eliza Segiet
Alicja Maria Kuberska * Teresa E. Gallion * Joe Paire
Kimberly Burnham * Shareef Abdur – Rasheed
Ashok K. Bhargava * Elizabeth Castillo * Swapna Behera
Tezmin Ition Tsai * William S. Peters, Sr.

Now Available

www.innerchildpress.com/the-year-of-the-poet

The Year of the Poet VI
May 2019

Featured Poets
Emad Al-Haydary * Hussein Nasser Jabr
Wahab Sheriff * Abdul Razzaq Al Ameeri

Asia Southeast Asia and Maritime Asia

The Poetry Posse 2019

Gail Weston Shazor * Albert Carrasco * Hülya N. Yılmaz
Jackie Davis Allen * Caroline Nazareno * Eliza Segiet
Alicja Maria Kubersla * Teresa E. Gallion * Joe Paire
Kimberly Burnham * Shareef Abdur – Rasheed
Ashok K. Bhargava * Elizabeth Castillo * Swapna Behera
Tezmin Ition Tsai * William S. Peters, Sr.

The Year of the Poet VI
June 2019

Featured Poets
Kate Gaudi Powiekszone * Sahaj Sabharwal
Iwu Jeff * Mohamed Abdel Aziz Shmeis

Arctic
Circumpolar

The Poetry Posse 2019

Gail Weston Shazor * Albert Carrasco * Hülya N. Yılmaz
Jackie Davis Allen * Caroline Nazareno * Eliza Segiet
Alicja Maria Kubersla * Teresa E. Gallion * Joe Paire
Kimberly Burnham * Shareef Abdur – Rasheed
Ashok K. Bhargava * Elizabeth Castillo * Swapna Behera
Tezmin Ition Tsai * William S. Peters, Sr.

The Year of the Poet VI
July 2019

Featured Poets
Saadeddin Shahin * Audy Scott
Fahreddin Shehu * Alok Kumar Ray

The Horn of Africa

Ethiopia   Djibouti

Somalia   Eritrea

The Poetry Posse 2019

Gail Weston Shazor * Albert Carrasco * Hülya N. Yılmaz
Jackie Davis Allen * Caroline Nazareno * Eliza Segiet
Alicja Maria Kubersla * Teresa E. Gallion * Joe Paire
Kimberly Burnham * Shareef Abdur – Rasheed
Ashok K. Bhargava * Elizabeth Castillo * Swapna Behera
Tezmin Ition Tsai * William S. Peters, Sr.

The Year of the Poet VI
August 2019

Featured Poets
Shola Balogun * Bharati Nayak
Monalisa Dash Dwibedy * Mbizo Chirasha

Coexist

Southwest Asia

The Poetry Posse 2019

Gail Weston Shazor * Albert Carrasco * Hülya N. Yılmaz
Jackie Davis Allen * Caroline Nazareno * Eliza Segiet
Alicja Maria Kubersla * Teresa E. Gallion * Joe Paire
Kimberly Burnham * Shareef Abdur – Rasheed
Ashok K. Bhargava * Elizabeth Castillo * Swapna Behera
Tezmin Ition Tsai * William S. Peters, Sr.

Now Available

www.innerchildpress.com/the-year-of-the-poet

225

The Year of the Poet VI

September 2019

Featured Poets

Elena Liliana Popescu * Gobinda Biswas
Irani Fatima 'Ashi' * Joseph S. Spence, Sr.

The Caucasus

The Poetry Posse 2019

Gail Weston Shazor * Albert Carrasco * Hülya N. Yılmaz
Jackie Davis Allen * Caroline Nazareno * Eliza Segiet
Alicja Maria Kuberska * Teresa E. Gallion * Joe Paire
Kimberly Burnham * Shareef Abdur ~ Rasheed
Ashok K. Bhargava * Elizabeth Castillo * Swapna Behera
Tezmin Ition Tsai * William S. Peters, Sr.

The Year of the Poet VI

October 2019

Featured Poets

Ngozi Olivia Osuoha * Denisa Kondic
Pankhuri Sinha * Christena AV Williams

The Nile Valley

The Poetry Posse 2019

Gail Weston Shazor * Albert Carrasco * Hülya N. Yılmaz
Jackie Davis Allen * Caroline Nazareno * Eliza Segiet
Alicja Maria Kuberska * Teresa E. Gallion * Joe Paire
Kimberly Burnham * Shareef Abdur ~ Rasheed
Ashok K. Bhargava * Elizabeth Castillo * Swapna Behera
Tezmin Ition Tsai * William S. Peters, Sr.

The Year of the Poet VI

November 2019

Featured Poets

Rozalia Aleksandrova * Orbindu Ganga
Smruti Ranjan Mohanty * Sofia Skleida

Northern Asia

The Poetry Posse 2019

Gail Weston Shazor * Albert Carrasco * Hülya N. Yılmaz
Jackie Davis Allen * Caroline Nazareno * Eliza Segiet
Alicja Maria Kuberska * Teresa E. Gallion * Joe Paire
Kimberly Burnham * Shareef Abdur ~ Rasheed
Ashok K. Bhargava * Elizabeth Castillo * Swapna Behera
Tezmin Ition Tsai * William S. Peters, Sr.

The Year of the Poet VI

December 2019

Featured Poets

Rabin Kumar (Karimov) * Sunny Paul
Bijayini Nayak * Kapardeli Eftichia

Oceania

The Poetry Posse 2019

Gail Weston Shazor * Albert Carrasco * Hülya N. Yılmaz
Jackie Davis Allen * Caroline Nazareno * Eliza Segiet
Alicja Maria Kuberska * Teresa E. Gallion * Joe Paire
Kimberly Burnham * Shareef Abdur ~ Rasheed
Ashok K. Bhargava * Elizabeth Castillo * Swapna Behera
Tezmin Ition Tsai * William S. Peters, Sr.

Now Available

www.innerchildpress.com/the-year-of-the-poet

The Year of the Poet VII

January 2020

Featured Poets

B S Tyagi * Ashok Chakravarthy Tholana
Andy Scott * Anwer Ghani

1901 Jean Henry Dunant and Frédéric Passy

The Year of Peace
Celebrating past Nobel Peace Prize Recipients

The Poetry Posse 2020

Gail Weston Shazor * Albert Carasco * Hülya N. Yılmaz
Jackie Davis Allen * Caroline Nazareno * Eliza Segiet
Alicja Maria Kuberska * Teresa E. Gallion * Joe Paire
Kimberly Burnham * Shareef Abdur – Rasheed
Ashok K. Bhargava * Elizabeth Castillo * Swapna Behera
Tezmin Ition Tsai * William S. Peters, Sr.

The Year of the Poet VII

February 2020

Featured Poets

Jennifer Ades * Martina Reisz Newberry
Ibrahim Honjo * Claudia Piccinno

Henri La Fontaine ~ 1913

The Year of Peace
Celebrating past Nobel Peace Prize Recipients

The Poetry Posse 2020

Gail Weston Shazor * Albert Carasco * Hülya N. Yılmaz
Jackie Davis Allen * Caroline Nazareno * Eliza Segiet
Alicja Maria Kuberska * Teresa E. Gallion * Joe Paire
Kimberly Burnham * Shareef Abdur – Rasheed
Ashok K. Bhargava * Elizabeth Castillo * Swapna Behera
Tezmin Ition Tsai * William S. Peters, Sr.

The Year of the Poet VII

March 2020

Featured Poets

Aziz Mountassir * Krishna Paraisa
Hannie Rouweler * Rozalia Aleksandrova

Aristide Briand ~ 1926 ~ Gustav Stresemann

The Year of Peace
Celebrating past Nobel Peace Prize Recipients

The Poetry Posse 2020

Gail Weston Shazor * Albert Carasco * Hülya N. Yılmaz
Jackie Davis Allen * Caroline Nazareno * Eliza Segiet
Alicja Maria Kuberska * Teresa E. Gallion * Joe Paire
Kimberly Burnham * Shareef Abdur – Rasheed
Ashok K. Bhargava * Elizabeth Castillo * Swapna Behera
Tezmin Ition Tsai * William S. Peters, Sr.

The Year of the Poet VII

April 2020

Featured Poets

Rohini Behera * Mircea Dan Duta
Monalisa Dash Dwibedy * NilavroNill Shoovro

Carlos Saavedra Lamas ~ 1936

The Year of Peace
Celebrating past Nobel Peace Prize Recipients

The Poetry Posse 2020

Gail Weston Shazor * Albert Carasco * Hülya N. Yılmaz
Jackie Davis Allen * Caroline Nazareno * Eliza Segiet
Alicja Maria Kuberska * Teresa E. Gallion * Joe Paire
Kimberly Burnham * Shareef Abdur – Rasheed
Ashok K. Bhargava * Elizabeth Castillo * Swapna Behera
Tezmin Ition Tsai * William S. Peters, Sr.

Now Available

www.innerchildpress.com/the-year-of-the-poet

The Year of the Poet VII
May 2020

Featured Poets
Alok Kumar Ray * Eden S. Trinidad
Franco Barbato * Izabela Zubko

Ralph Bunche ~ 1950

The Year of Peace
Celebrating past Nobel Peace Prize Recipients

The Poetry Posse 2020

Gail Weston Shazor * Albert Carasco * Hülya N. Yılmaz
Jackie Davis Allen * Caroline Nazareno * Eliza Segiet
Alicja Maria Kuberska * Teresa E. Gallion * Joe Paire
Kimberly Burnham * Shareef Abdur ~ Rasheed
Ashok K. Bhargava * Elizabeth Castillo * Swapna Behera
Tezmin Ition Tsai * William S. Peters, Sr.

The Year of the Poet VII
June 2020

Featured Poets
Eftichia Kapardeli * Metin Cengiz
Hussein Habasch * Kosh K Mathew

Albert John Lutuli ~ 1960

The Year of Peace
Celebrating past Nobel Peace Prize Recipients

The Poetry Posse 2020

Gail Weston Shazor * Albert Carasco * Hülya N. Yılmaz
Jackie Davis Allen * Caroline Nazareno * Eliza Segiet
Alicja Maria Kuberska * Teresa E. Gallion * Joe Paire
Kimberly Burnham * Shareef Abdur ~ Rasheed
Ashok K. Bhargava * Elizabeth Castillo * Swapna Behera
Tezmin Ition Tsai * William S. Peters, Sr.

The Year of the Poet VII
July 2020

Featured Poets
Mykola Martyniuk * Orbindu Ganga
Roula Pollard * Karn Praktisha

Norman Ernest Borlaug ~ 1970

The Year of Peace
Celebrating past Nobel Peace Prize Recipients

The Poetry Posse 2020

Gail Weston Shazor * Albert Carasco * Hülya N. Yılmaz
Jackie Davis Allen * Caroline Nazareno * Eliza Segiet
Alicja Maria Kuberska * Teresa E. Gallion * Joe Paire
Kimberly Burnham * Shareef Abdur ~ Rasheed
Ashok K. Bhargava * Elizabeth Castillo * Swapna Behera
Tezmin Ition Tsai * William S. Peters, Sr.

The Year of the Poet VII
August 2020

Featured Poets
Dr Pragya Suman * Chinh Nguyen
Srinivas Vasudev * Ugwu Leonard Ifeanyi, Jr.

Adolfo Pérez Esquivel ~ 1980

The Year of Peace
Celebrating past Nobel Peace Prize Recipients

The Poetry Posse 2020

Gail Weston Shazor * Albert Carasco * Hülya N. Yılmaz
Jackie Davis Allen * Caroline Nazareno * Eliza Segiet
Alicja Maria Kuberska * Teresa E. Gallion * Joe Paire
Kimberly Burnham * Shareef Abdur ~ Rasheed
Ashok K. Bhargava * Elizabeth Castillo * Swapna Behera
Tezmin Ition Tsai * William S. Peters, Sr.

Now Available

www.innerchildpress.com/the-year-of-the-poet

The Year of the Poet VII
September 2020
Featured Poets
Raed Anis Al-Jishi • Sotkonou Snehaa
Dr. Brajesh Kumar Gupta • Umid Najjari

Mikhail Sergeyevich Gorbachev ~ 1990

The Year of Peace
Celebrating past Nobel Peace Prize Recipients

The Poetry Posse 2020
Gail Weston Shazor • Albert Carasco • Hülya N. Yılmaz
Jackie Davis Allen • Caroline Nazareno • Eliza Segiet
Alicja Maria Kuberska • Teresa E. Gallion • Joe Paire
Kimberly Burnham • Shareef Abdur – Rasheed
Ashok K. Bhargava • Elizabeth Castillo • Swapna Behera
Tezmin Ition Tsai • William S. Peters, Sr.

The Year of the Poet VII
October 2020
Featured Poets
Mutawaf A. Shaheed • Galina Italyanskaya
Nadeem Fraz • Avril Tanya Meallem

Kim Dae-jung ~ 2000

The Year of Peace
Celebrating past Nobel Peace Prize Recipients

The Poetry Posse 2020
Gail Weston Shazor • Albert Carasco • Hülya N. Yılmaz
Jackie Davis Allen • Caroline Nazareno • Eliza Segiet
Alicja Maria Kuberska • Teresa E. Gallion • Joe Paire
Kimberly Burnham • Shareef Abdur – Rasheed
Ashok K. Bhargava • Elizabeth Castillo • Swapna Behera
Tezmin Ition Tsai • William S. Peters, Sr.

The Year of the Poet VII
November 2020
Featured Poets
Elisa Mascia • Sue Dudenberg McClelland
Hatif Janabi • Ivan Gacina

Liu Xiaobo ~ 2010

The Year of Peace
Celebrating past Nobel Peace Prize Recipients

The Poetry Posse 2020
Gail Weston Shazor • Albert Carasco • Hülya N. Yılmaz
Jackie Davis Allen • Caroline Nazareno • Eliza Segiet
Alicja Maria Kuberska • Teresa E. Gallion • Joe Paire
Kimberly Burnham • Shareef Abdur – Rasheed
Ashok K. Bhargava • Elizabeth Castillo • Swapna Behera
Tezmin Ition Tsai • William S. Peters, Sr.

The Year of the Poet VII
December 2020
Featured Poets
Ratan Ghosh • Ibtisam Ibrahim Al-Asady
Brindha Vinodh • Selma Kopic

Abiy Ahmed Ali ~ 2019

The Year of Peace
Celebrating past Nobel Peace Prize Recipients

The Poetry Posse 2020
Gail Weston Shazor • Albert Carasco • Hülya N. Yılmaz
Jackie Davis Allen • Caroline Nazareno • Eliza Segiet
Alicja Maria Kuberska • Teresa E. Gallion • Joe Paire
Kimberly Burnham • Shareef Abdur – Rasheed
Ashok K. Bhargava • Elizabeth Castillo • Swapna Behera
Tezmin Ition Tsai • William S. Peters, Sr.

Now Available

www.innerchildpress.com/the-year-of-the-poet

The Year of the Poet VIII

January 2021

Featured Global Poets

Andrew Scott * Debaprasanna Biswas
Shakil Kalam * Changming Yuan

Banksy's The Girl with the Pierced Eardrum

Poetry ... Ekphrasticly Speaking

The Poetry Posse 2020

Gail Weston Shazor * Albert Carasico * Hülya N. Yılmaz
Jackie Davis Allen * Caroline Nazareno * Eliza Segiet
Alicja Maria Kuberska * Teresa E. Gallion * Joe Paire
Kimberly Burnham * Shareef Abdur – Rasheed
Ashok K. Bhargava * Elizabeth Castillo * Swapna Behera
Tezmin Ition Tsai * William S. Peters, Sr.

The Year of the Poet VIII

February 2021

Featured Global Poets

T. Ramesh Babu * Ruchida Barman

Neptune Barman * Faleeha Hassan

Emory Douglas : 1968 Olympics mural

Poetry ... Ekphrasticly Speaking

The Poetry Posse 2021

Gail Weston Shazor * Albert Carasico * Hülya N. Yılmaz
Jackie Davis Allen * Caroline Nazareno * Eliza Segiet
Alicja Maria Kuberska * Teresa E. Gallion * Joe Paire
Kimberly Burnham * Shareef Abdur – Rasheed
Ashok K. Bhargava * Elizabeth Castillo * Swapna Behera
Tezmin Ition Tsai * William S. Peters, Sr.

The Year of the Poet VIII

March 2021

Featured Global Poets

Claudia Piccinno * Mohammed Jabr
Luzviminda Rivera *Nigar Arif

Tatyana Fazlalizadeh

Poetry ... Ekphrasticly Speaking

The Poetry Posse 2021

Gail Weston Shazor * Albert Carasico * Hülya N. Yılmaz
Jackie Davis Allen * Caroline Nazareno * Eliza Segiet
Alicja Maria Kuberska * Teresa E. Gallion * Joe Paire
Kimberly Burnham * Shareef Abdur – Rasheed
Ashok K. Bhargava * Elizabeth Castillo * Swapna Behera
Tezmin Ition Tsai * William S. Peters, Sr.

The Year of the Poet VIII

April 2021

Featured Global Poets

Katarzyna Brus- Sawczuk * Anwesha Paul
Rozalia Aleksandrova * Shahid Abbas

Pablo O'Higgins

Poetry ... Ekphrasticly Speaking

The Poetry Posse 2021

Gail Weston Shazor * Albert Carasico * Hülya N. Yılmaz
Jackie Davis Allen * Caroline Nazareno * Eliza Segiet
Alicja Maria Kuberska * Teresa E. Gallion * Joe Paire
Kimberly Burnham * Shareef Abdur – Rasheed
Ashok K. Bhargava * Elizabeth Castillo * Swapna Behera
Tezmin Ition Tsai * William S. Peters, Sr.

Now Available

www.innerchildpress.com/the-year-of-the-poet

The Year of the Poet VIII
May 2021
Featured Global Poets
Paramita Mukherjee Mullick * Rose Zerguine
Jaydeep Sarangi * Bismay Mohanty

Diego Rivera

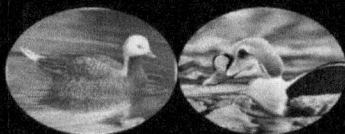

Poetry . . . Ekphrasticly Speaking
The Poetry Posse 2021
Gail Weston Shazor * Albert Carasco * Hülya N. Yılmaz
Jackie Davis Allen * Caroline Nazareno * Eliza Segiet
Alicja Maria Kuberska * Teresa E. Gallion * Joe Paire
Kimberly Burnham * Shareef Abdur – Rasheed
Ashok K. Bhargava * Elizabeth Castillo * Swapna Behera
Tezmin Ition Tsai * William S. Peters, Sr.

The Year of the Poet VIII
June 2021
Featured Global Poets
Alonzo "zO" Gross * Lali Tsipi Michaeli
Tareq al Karmy * Tirthendu Ganguly

Rayen Kang

Poetry . . . Ekphrasticly Speaking
The Poetry Posse 2021
Gail Weston Shazor * Albert Carasco * Hülya N. Yılmaz
Jackie Davis Allen * Caroline Nazareno * Eliza Segiet
Alicja Maria Kuberska * Teresa E. Gallion * Joe Paire
Kimberly Burnham * Shareef Abdur – Rasheed
Ashok K. Bhargava * Elizabeth Castillo * Swapna Behera
Tezmin Ition Tsai * William S. Peters, Sr.

The Year of the Poet VIII
July 2021
Featured Global Poets
Iram Jaan * Vesna Mundishevska-Veljanovska
Ngozi Olivia Osuoha * Lan Qyqalla

Goncalao Mabunda

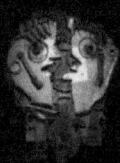

Poetry . . . Ekphrasticly Speaking
The Poetry Posse 2021
Gail Weston Shazor * Albert Carasco * Hülya N. Yılmaz
Jackie Davis Allen * Caroline Nazareno * Eliza Segiet
Alicja Maria Kuberska * Teresa E. Gallion * Joe Paire
Kimberly Burnham * Shareef Abdur – Rasheed
Ashok K. Bhargava * Elizabeth Castillo * Swapna Behera
Tezmin Ition Tsai * William S. Peters, Sr.

The Year of the Poet VIII
August 2021
Featured Global Poets
Caroline Laurent Turunc * Kamal Dhungana
Pankhuri Sinha * Paramita Mukherjee Mullick

Mundara Koorang

Poetry . . . Ekphrasticly Speaking
The Poetry Posse 2021
Gail Weston Shazor * Albert Carasco * Hülya N. Yılmaz
Jackie Davis Allen * Caroline Nazareno * Eliza Segiet
Alicja Maria Kuberska * Teresa E. Gallion * Joe Paire
Kimberly Burnham * Shareef Abdur – Rasheed
Ashok K. Bhargava * Elizabeth Castillo * Swapna Behera
Tezmin Ition Tsai * William S. Peters, Sr.

Now Available
www.innerchildpress.com/the-year-of-the-poet

The Year of the Poet VIII

September 2021

Featured Global Poets

Monsif Beroual * Sandesh Ghimire

Sharmila Poudel * Pavol Janik

Heather Jansch

Poetry . . . Ekphrasticly Speaking

The Poetry Posse 2021

Gail Weston Shazor * Albert Carasso * Hülya N. Yılmaz
Jackie Davis Allen * Caroline Nazareno * Eliza Segiet
Alicja Maria Kuberska * Teresa E. Gallion * Joe Paire
Kimberly Burnham * Shareef Abdur – Rasheed
Ashok K. Bhargava * Elizabeth Castillo * Swapna Behera
Tezmin Ition Tsai * William S. Peters, Sr.

The Year of the Poet VIII

October 2021

Featured Global Poets

C. E. Shy * Saswata Ganguly
Suranjit Gain * Hasiba Hilal

Dale Lamphere

Poetry . . . Ekphrasticly Speaking

The Poetry Posse 2021

Gail Weston Shazor * Albert Carasso * Hülya N. Yılmaz
Jackie Davis Allen * Caroline Nazareno * Eliza Segiet
Alicja Maria Kuberska * Teresa E. Gallion * Joe Paire
Kimberly Burnham * Shareef Abdur – Rasheed
Ashok K. Bhargava * Elizabeth Castillo * Swapna Behera
Tezmin Ition Tsai * William S. Peters, Sr.

The Year of the Poet VIII

November 2021

Featured Global Poets

Errol D. Bean * Ibrahim Honjo
Tanja Ajtic * Rajashree Mohapatra

Andy Goldsworthy

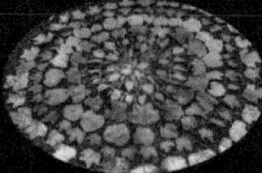

Poetry . . . Ekphrasticly Speaking

The Poetry Posse 2021

Gail Weston Shazor * Albert Carasso * Hülya N. Yılmaz
Jackie Davis Allen * Caroline Nazareno * Eliza Segiet
Alicja Maria Kuberska * Teresa E. Gallion * Joe Paire
Kimberly Burnham * Shareef Abdur – Rasheed
Ashok K. Bhargava * Elizabeth Castillo * Swapna Behera
Tezmin Ition Tsai * William S. Peters, Sr.

The Year of the Poet VIII

December 2021

Featured Global Poets

Orbinda Ganga * Fadairo Tesleem
Anthony Arnold * Iyad Shamasnah

Fredric Edwin Church

Poetry . . . Ekphrasticly Speaking

The Poetry Posse 2021

Gail Weston Shazor * Albert Carasso * Hülya N. Yılmaz
Jackie Davis Allen * Caroline Nazareno * Eliza Segiet
Alicja Maria Kuberska * Teresa E. Gallion * Joe Paire
Kimberly Burnham * Shareef Abdur – Rasheed
Ashok K. Bhargava * Elizabeth Castillo * Swapna Behera
Tezmin Ition Tsai * William S. Peters, Sr.

Now Available

www.innerchildpress.com/the-year-of-the-poet

The Year of the Poet IX
January 2022

Featured Global Poets
**Ratan Ghosh * Christine Neil-Wright
Andrew Scott * Ashok Kumar**

Climate Change : The Ice Cap

Poetry . . . Ekphrasticly Speaking

The Poetry Posse 2021

Gail Weston Shazor * Albert Carassco * Hülya N. Yilmaz
Jackie Davis Allen * Caroline Nazareno * Eliza Segiet
Alicja Maria Kubeska * Teresa E. Gallion * Joe Paire
Kimberly Burnham * Shareef Abdur – Rasheed
Ashok K. Bhargava * Elizabeth Castillo * Swapna Behera
Tezmin Ition Tsai * William S. Peters, Sr.

The Year of the Poet IX
February 2022

Featured Global Poets
Roza Boyanova * Ramón de Jesús Núñez Duval
Mammad Ismayil * Tarana Turan Rahimli

Climate Change and Mountains

Poetry . . . Ekphrasticly Speaking

The Poetry Posse 2021

Gail Weston Shazor * Albert Carassco * Hülya N. Yilmaz
Jackie Davis Allen * Caroline Nazareno * Eliza Segiet
Alicja Maria Kubeska * Teresa E. Gallion * Joe Paire
Kimberly Burnham * Shareef Abdur – Rasheed
Ashok K. Bhargava * Elizabeth Castillo * Swapna Behera
Tezmin Ition Tsai * William S. Peters, Sr.

The Year of the Poet IX
March 2022

Featured Global Poets
Dimitris P. Kraniotis * Marlene Pasini
Kennedy Ochieng * Swayam Prashant

Climate Change and Space Debris

Poetry . . . Ekphrasticly Speaking

The Poetry Posse 2021

Gail Weston Shazor * Albert Carassco * Hülya N. Yilmaz
Jackie Davis Allen * Caroline Nazareno * Eliza Segiet
Alicja Maria Kubeska * Teresa E. Gallion * Joe Paire
Kimberly Burnham * Shareef Abdur – Rasheed
Ashok K. Bhargava * Elizabeth Castillo * Swapna Behera
Tezmin Ition Tsai * William S. Peters, Sr.

The Year of the Poet IX
April 2022

Featured Global Poets
**Alonzo Gross * Dr. Debaprasanna Biswas
Monsif Beroual * Carol Aronoff**

Climate Change and Oceans

***Celebrating our 100th Edition ***

Poetry . . . Ekphrasticly Speaking

The Poetry Posse 2021

Gail Weston Shazor * Albert Carassco * Hülya N. Yilmaz
Jackie Davis Allen * Caroline Nazareno * Eliza Segiet
Alicja Maria Kubeska * Teresa E. Gallion * Joe Paire
Kimberly Burnham * Shareef Abdur – Rasheed
Ashok K. Bhargava * Elizabeth Castillo * Swapna Behera
Tezmin Ition Tsai * William S. Peters, Sr.

Now Available

www.innerchildpress.com/the-year-of-the-poet

The Year of the Poet IX
May 2022

Featured Global Poets

Ndaba Sibanda * Smrutiranjan Mohanty
Ajanta Paul * Monalisa Dash Dwibedy

Climate Change and Birds

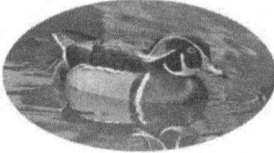

Poetry . . . Ekphrasticly Speaking

The Poetry Posse 2021

Gail Weston Shazor * Albert Carasco * Hülya N. Yılmaz
Jackie Davis Allen * Caroline Nazareno * Eliza Segiet
Alicja Maria Kuberska * Teresa E. Gallion * Joe Paire
Kimberly Burnham * Shareef Abdur – Rasheed
Ashok K. Bhargava * Elizabeth Castillo * Swapna Behera
Tezmin Ition Tsai * William S. Peters, Sr.

The Year of the Poet IX
June 2022

Featured Global Poets

Yuan Changming * Azeezat Okunlola
Tanja Ajtié * Philip Chijioke Abonyi

Climate Change and Trees

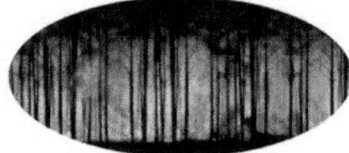

Poetry . . . Ekphrasticly Speaking

The Poetry Posse 2022

Gail Weston Shazor * Albert Carasco * Hülya N. Yılmaz
Jackie Davis Allen * Caroline Nazareno * Eliza Segiet
Alicja Maria Kuberska * Teresa E. Gallion * Joe Paire
Kimberly Burnham * Shareef Abdur – Rasheed
Ashok K. Bhargava * Elizabeth Castillo * Swapna Behera
Tezmin Ition Tsai * William S. Peters, Sr.

The Year of the Poet IX
July 2022

Featured Global Poets

Michelle Joan Barulich * Mili Das
Anna Ferriero * Ujjal Mandal

Climate Change and Animals

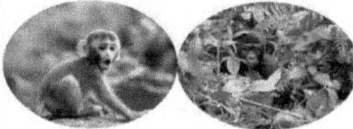

Poetry . . . Ekphrasticly Speaking

The Poetry Posse 2022

Gail Weston Shazor * Albert Carasco * Hülya N. Yılmaz
Jackie Davis Allen * Caroline Nazareno * Eliza Segiet
Alicja Maria Kuberska * Teresa E. Gallion * Joe Paire
Kimberly Burnham * Shareef Abdur – Rasheed
Ashok K. Bhargava * Elizabeth Castillo * Swapna Behera
Tezmin Ition Tsai * William S. Peters, Sr.

The Year of the Poet IX
August 2022

Featured Global Poets

Pankhuri Sinha * Abdulloh Abdumominov
Caroline Turunç * Tali Cohen Shabtai

Climate Change and Agriculture

Poetry . . . Ekphrasticly Speaking

The Poetry Posse 2022

Gail Weston Shazor * Albert Carasco * Hülya N. Yılmaz
Jackie Davis Allen * Caroline Nazareno * Eliza Segiet
Alicja Maria Kuberska * Teresa E. Gallion * Joe Paire
Kimberly Burnham * Shareef Abdur – Rasheed
Ashok K. Bhargava * Elizabeth Castillo * Swapna Behera
Tezmin Ition Tsai * William S. Peters, Sr.

Now Available

www.innerchildpress.com/the-year-of-the-poet

The Year of the Poet IX
September 2022

Featured Global Poets
**Ngozi Olivia Osuoha * Biswajit Mishra
Sylwia K. Malinowska * Sajid Hussein**

Climate Change and Wind and Weather Patterns

Poetry . . . Ekphrasticly Speaking

The Poetry Posse 2022

Gail Weston Shazor * Albert Carasco * Hülya N. Yılmaz
Jackie Davis Allen * Caroline Nazareno * Eliza Segiet
Alicja Maria Kubenska * Teresa E. Gallion * Joe Paire
Kimberly Burnham * Shareef Abdur – Rasheed
Ashok K. Bhargava * Elizabeth Castillo * Swapna Behera
Tezmin Ition Tsai * William S. Peters, Sr.

The Year of the Poet IX
October 2022

Featured Global Poets
**Andrew Kouroupos * Brenda Mohammed
Carthornia Kouroupos * Faleeha Hassan**

Climate Change and Oil and Power

Poetry . . . Ekphrasticly Speaking

The Poetry Posse 2022

Gail Weston Shazor * Albert Carasco * Hülya N. Yılmaz
Jackie Davis Allen * Caroline Nazareno * Eliza Segiet
Alicja Maria Kubenska * Teresa E. Gallion * Joe Paire
Kimberly Burnham * Shareef Abdur – Rasheed
Ashok K. Bhargava * Elizabeth Castillo * Swapna Behera
Tezmin Ition Tsai * William S. Peters, Sr.

The Year of the Poet IX
November 2022

Featured Global Poets
**Hema Ravi * Shafkat Aziz Hajam
Selma Kopic * Ibrahim Honjo**

Climate Change : Time to Act

Poetry . . . Ekphrasticly Speaking

The Poetry Posse 2022

Gail Weston Shazor * Albert Carasco * Hülya N. Yılmaz
Jackie Davis Allen * Caroline Nazareno * Eliza Segiet
Alicja Maria Kubenska * Teresa E. Gallion * Joe Paire
Kimberly Burnham * Shareef Abdur – Rasheed
Ashok K. Bhargava * Elizabeth Castillo * Swapna Behera
Tezmin Ition Tsai * William S. Peters, Sr.

The Year of the Poet IX
December 2022

Featured Global Poets
**Elarbi Abdelfattah * Lorraine Cragg
Neha Bhandarkar * Robert Gibbons**

Climate Change Bees, Butterflies and Insect Life

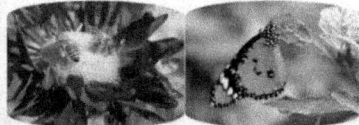

Poetry . . . Ekphrasticly Speaking

The Poetry Posse 2022

Gail Weston Shazor * Albert Carasco * Hülya N. Yılmaz
Jackie Davis Allen * Caroline Nazareno * Eliza Segiet
Alicja Maria Kubenska * Teresa E. Gallion * Joe Paire
Kimberly Burnham * Shareef Abdur – Rasheed
Ashok K. Bhargava * Elizabeth Castillo * Swapna Behera
Tezmin Ition Tsai * William S. Peters, Sr.

Now Available

www.innerchildpress.com/the-year-of-the-poet

The Year of the Poet X
January 2023

Featured Global Poets

JuNe Barefield * Swayam Prashant
Willow Rose * Shabbirhusein K Jamnagerwalla

Children: Difference Makers

Iqbal Masih

The Poetry Posse 2023

Gail Weston Shazor * Albert Carassco * Hülya N. Yılmaz
Jackie Davis Allen * Caroline Nazareno * Kimberly Burnham
Alicja Maria Kuberska * Teresa E. Gallion * Joe Paire
Michelle Joan Barulich * Shareef Abdur – Rasheed
Ashok K. Bhargava * Elizabeth Castillo * Swapna Behera
Tezmin Ition Tsai * Eliza Segiet * William S. Peters, Sr.

The Year of the Poet X
February 2023

Featured Global Poets

Christena Williams * Hilda Graciela Kraft
Francesco Favetta * Dr. H.C. Louise Hudon

Children : Difference Makers

Ruby Bridges

The Poetry Posse 2023

Gail Weston Shazor * Albert Carassco * Hülya N. Yılmaz
Jackie Davis Allen * Caroline Nazareno * Kimberly Burnham
Alicja Maria Kuberska * Teresa E. Gallion * Joe Paire
Michelle Joan Barulich * Shareef Abdur – Rasheed
Ashok K. Bhargava * Elizabeth Castillo * Swapna Behera
Tezmin Ition Tsai * Eliza Segiet * William S. Peters, Sr.

The Year of the Poet X
March 2023

Featured Global Poets

Clarena Martínez Turizo * Binod Dawadi
Til Kumari Sharma * Petrouchka Alexieva

Children : Difference Makers

Yo Yo Ma

The Poetry Posse 2023

Gail Weston Shazor * Albert Carassco * Hülya N. Yılmaz
Jackie Davis Allen * Caroline Nazareno * Kimberly Burnham
Alicja Maria Kuberska * Teresa E. Gallion * Joe Paire
Michelle Joan Barulich * Shareef Abdur – Rasheed
Ashok K. Bhargava * Elizabeth Castillo * Swapna Behera
Tezmin Ition Tsai * Eliza Segiet * William S. Peters, Sr.

The Year of the Poet X
April 2023

Featured Global Poets

Maxwanette A Poetess * Alonzo Gross
Türkan Ergör * Ibrahim Honjo

Children : Difference Makers

Claudette Colvin

The Poetry Posse 2023

Gail Weston Shazor * Albert Carassco * Hülya N. Yılmaz
Jackie Davis Allen * Caroline Nazareno * Kimberly Burnham
Alicja Maria Kuberska * Teresa E. Gallion * Joe Paire
Michelle Joan Barulich * Shareef Abdur – Rasheed
Ashok K. Bhargava * Elizabeth Castillo * Swapna Behera
Tezmin Ition Tsai * Eliza Segiet * William S. Peters, Sr.

Now Available

www.innerchildpress.com/the-year-of-the-poet

The Year of the Poet X
May 2023

Csp Shrivastava * Michael Lee Johnson
Taghrid Bou Merhi * Yasmin Brown

Children : Difference Makers

Louis Braille

The Poetry Posse 2023

Gail Weston Shazor * Albert Carasco * Hülya N. Yılmaz
Jackie Davis Allen * Caroline Nazareno * Kimberly Burnham
Alicja Maria Kuberska * Teresa E. Gallion * Joe Paire
Michelle Joan Barulich * Shareef Abdur – Rasheed
Ashok K. Bhargava * Elizabeth Castillo * Swapna Behera
Tezmin Ition Tsai * Eliza Segiet * William S. Peters, Sr.

The Year of the Poet X
June 2023

Featured Global Poets

Kay Peters · Carthornia Kouroupos
Andrew Kouroupos · Faleeha Hassan

Children : Difference Makers

Ryan Hreljac

The Poetry Posse 2023

Gail Weston Shazor * Albert Carasco * Hülya N. Yılmaz
Jackie Davis Allen * Caroline Nazareno * Kimberly Burnham
Alicja Maria Kuberska * Teresa E. Gallion * Joe Paire
Michelle Joan Barulich * Shareef Abdur – Rasheed
Ashok K. Bhargava * Elizabeth Castillo * Swapna Behera
Tezmin Ition Tsai * Eliza Segiet * William S. Peters, Sr.

The Year of the Poet X
July 2023

Featured Global Poets

Rajashree Mohapatra * Biswajit Mishra
Johan Karlsson * Teodozja Swiderska

Children : Difference Makers

~ Bana al-Abed ~

The Poetry Posse 2023

Gail Weston Shazor * Albert Carasco * Hülya N. Yılmaz
Jackie Davis Allen * Caroline Nazareno * Kimberly Burnham
Alicja Maria Kuberska * Teresa E. Gallion * Joe Paire
Michelle Joan Barulich * Shareef Abdur – Rasheed
Ashok K. Bhargava * Elizabeth Castillo * Swapna Behera
Tezmin Ition Tsai * Eliza Segiet * William S. Peters, Sr.

The Year of the Poet X
August 2023

Featured Global Poets

Kennedy Wanda Ochieng * Jose Lopez
Sylwia K. Malinowska * Laurent Grison

Children : Difference Makers

~ Kelvin Doe ~

The Poetry Posse 2023

Gail Weston Shazor * Albert Carasco * Hülya N. Yılmaz
Jackie Davis Allen * Caroline Nazareno * Kimberly Burnham
Alicja Maria Kuberska * Teresa E. Gallion * Joe Paire
Michelle Joan Barulich * Shareef Abdur – Rasheed
Ashok K. Bhargava * Elizabeth Castillo * Swapna Behera
Tezmin Ition Tsai * Eliza Segiet * William S. Peters, Sr.

Now Available

www.innerchildpress.com/the-year-of-the-poet

The Year of the Poet X
September 2023

Featured Global Poets
Eftichia Karpadeli * Chinh Nguyen
Nigar Agalarova * Carmela Cueva

Children : Difference Makers

~ Easton LaChappelle ~

The Poetry Posse 2023

Gail Weston Shazor * Albert Carasco * Hülya N. Yılmaz
Jackie Davis Allen * Caroline Nazareno * Kimberly Burnham
Alicja Maria Kuberska * Teresa E. Gallion * Joe Paire
Michelle Joan Barulich * Shareef Abdur – Rasheed
Ashok K. Bhargava * Elizabeth Castillo * Swapna Behera
Tezmin Ition Tsai * Eliza Segiet * William S. Peters, Sr.

The Year of the Poet X
October 2023

Featured Global Poets
CSP Shrivastava * Huniie Parker
Noreen Snyder * Ramkrishna Paul

Children : Difference Makers

~ Malala Yousafzai ~

The Poetry Posse 2023

Gail Weston Shazor * Albert Carasco * Hülya N. Yılmaz
Jackie Davis Allen * Caroline Nazareno * Kimberly Burnham
Alicja Maria Kuberska * Teresa E. Gallion * Joe Paire
Michelle Joan Barulich * Shareef Abdur – Rasheed
Ashok K. Bhargava * Elizabeth Castillo * Swapna Behera
Tezmin Ition Tsai * Eliza Segiet * William S. Peters, Sr.

The Year of the Poet X
November 2023

Featured Global Poets
Ibrahim Honjo * Balachandran Nair
Xanthi Hondrou-Hil * Francesco Favetta

Children : Difference Makers

~ Jean-Michel Basquiat ~

The Poetry Posse 2023

Gail Weston Shazor * Albert Carasco * Hülya N. Yılmaz
Jackie Davis Allen * Caroline Nazareno * Kimberly Burnham
Alicja Maria Kuberska * Teresa E. Gallion * Joe Paire
Michelle Joan Barulich * Shareef Abdur – Rasheed
Ashok K. Bhargava * Elizabeth Castillo * Swapna Behera
Tezmin Ition Tsai * Eliza Segiet * William S. Peters, Sr.

The Year of the Poet X
December 2023

Featured Global Poets
Caroline Laurent Turunc * Neha Bhandarkar
Shafkat Aziz Hajam * Elarbi Abdelfattah

Children : Difference Makers

~ Melati and Isabel Wijsen ~

The Poetry Posse 2023

Gail Weston Shazor * Albert Carasco * Hülya N. Yılmaz
Jackie Davis Allen * Caroline Nazareno * Kimberly Burnham
Alicja Maria Kuberska * Teresa E. Gallion * Joe Paire
Michelle Joan Barulich * Shareef Abdur – Rasheed
Ashok K. Bhargava * Elizabeth Castillo * Swapna Behera
Tezmin Ition Tsai * Eliza Segiet * William S. Peters, Sr.

Now Available

www.innerchildpress.com/the-year-of-the-poet

The Year of the Poet XI
January 2024

Featured Global Poets

Til Kumari Sharma * Shafkat Aziz Hajam
Daniela Marian * Eleni Vassiliou – Asteroskon

Renowned Poets

~ Phyllis Wheatley ~

The Poetry Posse 2024

Gail Weston Shazor * Albert Carasco * Hülya N. Yılmaz
Jackie Davis Allen * Caroline Nazareno * Mutawaf Shaheed
Alicja Maria Kuberska * Teresa E. Gallion * Noreen Snyder
Michelle Joan Barulich * Shareef Abdur – Rasheed
Ashok K. Bhargava * Elizabeth Castillo * Swapna Behera
Tezmin Ition Tsai * Eliza Segiet * William S. Peters, Sr.

The Year of the Poet XI
February 2024

Featured Global Poets

Caroline Laurent Turunç * Julio Pavanetti
Lidia Chiarelli * Lina Buividavičiūtė

Renowned Poets

~ Omar Khayyam ~

The Poetry Posse 2024

Gail Weston Shazor * Albert Carasco * Hülya N. Yılmaz
Jackie Davis Allen * Caroline Nazareno * Mutawaf Shaheed
Alicja Maria Kuberska * Teresa E. Gallion * Noreen Snyder
Michelle Joan Barulich * Shareef Abdur – Rasheed
Ashok K. Bhargava * Elizabeth Castillo * Swapna Behera
Tezmin Ition Tsai * Eliza Segiet * William S. Peters, Sr.

The Year of the Poet XI
March 2024

Featured Global Poets

Francesco Favetta * Jagjit Singh Zandu
Carmela Núñez Yukimura Peruana * Michael Lee Johnson

Renowned Poets

~ Nâzim Hikmet ~

The Poetry Posse 2024

Gail Weston Shazor * Albert Carasco * Hülya N. Yılmaz
Jackie Davis Allen * Caroline Nazareno * Mutawaf Shaheed
Alicja Maria Kuberska * Teresa E. Gallion * Noreen Snyder
Michelle Joan Barulich * Shareef Abdur – Rasheed
Ashok K. Bhargava * Elizabeth Castillo * Swapna Behera
Tezmin Ition Tsai * Eliza Segiet * William S. Peters, Sr.

The Year of the Poet XI
April 2024

Featured Global Poets

Hassanal Abdullah * Johny Takkedasila
Rajashree Mohapatra * Shirley Smothers

Renowned Poets

~ William Butler Yeats ~

The Poetry Posse 2024

Gail Weston Shazor * Albert Carasco * Hülya N. Yılmaz
Jackie Davis Allen * Caroline Nazareno * Mutawaf Shaheed
Alicja Maria Kuberska * Teresa E. Gallion * Noreen Snyder
Michelle Joan Barulich * Shareef Abdur – Rasheed
Ashok K. Bhargava * Elizabeth Castillo * Swapna Behera
Tezmin Ition Tsai * Eliza Segiet * William S. Peters, Sr.

Now Available

www.innerchildpress.com/the-year-of-the-poet

The Year of the Poet XI
May 2024

Featured Global Poets

Binod Dawadi * Petros Kyriakou Veloudas
Rayees Ahmad Kumar * Solomon C Jatta

Renowned Poets

~ Makhanlal Chaturvedi ~

The Poetry Posse 2024

Gail Weston Shazor * Albert Carasco * Hülya N. Yılmaz
Jackie Davis Allen * Caroline Nazareno * Mutawaf Shaheed
Alicja Maria Kuberska * Teresa E. Gallion * Noreen Snyder
Michelle Joan Barulich * Shareef Abdur – Rasheed
Ashok K. Bhargava * Elizabeth Castillo * Swapna Behera
Tezmin Ition Tsai * Eliza Segiet * William S. Peters, Sr.

The Year of the Poet XI
June 2024

Featured Global Poets

C. S. P Shrivastava * Maria Evelyn Quilla Soleta
Moulay Cherif Chebihi Hassani * Swayam Prashant

Renowned Poets

~ Langston Hughs ~

The Poetry Posse 2024

Gail Weston Shazor * Albert Carasco * Hülya N. Yılmaz
Jackie Davis Allen * Caroline Nazareno * Mutawaf Shaheed
Alicja Maria Kuberska * Teresa E. Gallion * Noreen Snyder
Michelle Joan Barulich * Shareef Abdur – Rasheed
Ashok K. Bhargava * Elizabeth Castillo * Swapna Behera
Tezmin Ition Tsai * Eliza Segiet * William S. Peters, Sr.

The Year of the Poet XI
July 2024

Featured Global Poets

Barbara Gaiardoni * Bharati Nayak
Errol Bean * Michael Lee Johnson

Renowned Poets

~ Pablo Neruda ~

The Poetry Posse 2024

Gail Weston Shazor * Albert Carasco * Hülya N. Yılmaz
Jackie Davis Allen * Caroline Nazareno * Mutawaf Shaheed
Alicja Maria Kuberska * Teresa E. Gallion * Noreen Snyder
Michelle Joan Barulich * Shareef Abdur – Rasheed
Ashok K. Bhargava * Elizabeth Castillo * Swapna Behera
Tezmin Ition Tsai * Eliza Segiet * William S. Peters, Sr.

The Year of the Poet XI
August 2024

Featured Global Poets

Ibrahim Honjo * Khalice Jade
Irma Kurti * Mennadi Farah

Renowned Poets

~ Li Bai ~

The Poetry Posse 2024

Gail Weston Shazor * Albert Carasco * Hülya N. Yılmaz
Jackie Davis Allen * Caroline Nazareno * Mutawaf Shaheed
Alicja Maria Kuberska * Teresa E. Gallion * Noreen Snyder
Michelle Joan Barulich * Shareef Abdur – Rasheed
Ashok K. Bhargava * Elizabeth Castillo * Swapna Behera
Tezmin Ition Tsai * Eliza Segiet * William S. Peters, Sr.

Now Available

www.innerchildpress.com/the-year-of-the-poet

The Year of the Poet XI
September 2024

Featured Global Poets

Ngozi Olivia Osuoha * Teodozja Świderska
Chinh Nguyen * Awatef El Idrissi Boukhris

Renowned Poets

~ William Ernest Henley ~
The Poetry Posse 2024

Gail Weston Shazor * Albert Carasco * Hülya N. Yılmaz
Jackie Davis Allen * Caroline Nazareno * Mutawaf Shaheed
Alicja Maria Kuberska * Teresa E. Gallion * Noreen Snyder
Michelle Joan Barulich * Shareef Abdur – Rasheed
Ashok K. Bhargava * Elizabeth Castillo * Swapna Behera
Tezmin Ition Tsai * Eliza Segiet * William S. Peters, Sr.

The Year of the Poet XI
October 2024

Featured Global Poets

Deepak Kumar Dey * Shallal 'Anouz
Adnan Al-Sayegh * Taghrid Bou Merhi

Renowned Poets

~ Adam Mickiewicz ~
The Poetry Posse 2024

Gail Weston Shazor * Albert Carasco * Hülya N. Yılmaz
Jackie Davis Allen * Caroline Nazareno * Mutawaf Shaheed
Alicja Maria Kuberska * Teresa E. Gallion * Noreen Snyder
Michelle Joan Barulich * Shareef Abdur – Rasheed
Ashok K. Bhargava * Elizabeth Castillo * Swapna Behera
Tezmin Ition Tsai * Eliza Segiet * William S. Peters, Sr.

The Year of the Poet XI
November 2024

Featured Global Poets

Abraham Tawiah Tei * Neha Bhandarkar
Zaneta Varnado Johns * Haseena Bnaiyan

Renowned Poets

~ Wole Soyinka ~
The Poetry Posse 2024

Gail Weston Shazor * Albert Carasco * Hülya N. Yılmaz
Jackie Davis Allen * Caroline Nazareno * Mutawaf Shaheed
Alicja Maria Kuberska * Teresa E. Gallion * Noreen Snyder
Michelle Joan Barulich * Shareef Abdur – Rasheed
Ashok K. Bhargava * Elizabeth Castillo * Swapna Behera
Tezmin Ition Tsai * Eliza Segiet * William S. Peters, Sr.

The Year of the Poet XI
December 2024

Featured Global Poets

Kapardeli Eftichia * Irena Jovanović
Sudipta Mishra * Til Kumari Sharma

Renowned Poets

~ Imru' al-Qais ~
The Poetry Posse 2024

Gail Weston Shazor * Albert Carasco * Hülya N. Yılmaz
Jackie Davis Allen * Caroline Nazareno * Mutawaf Shaheed
Alicja Maria Kuberska * Teresa E. Gallion * Noreen Snyder
Michelle Joan Barulich * Shareef Abdur – Rasheed * Swapna Behera
Ashok K. Bhargava * Elizabeth Castillo * Kimberly Burnham
Tezmin Ition Tsai * Eliza Segiet * William S. Peters, Sr.

Now Available

www.innerchildpress.com/the-year-of-the-poet

The Year of the Poet XII
January 2025

Featured Global Poets

Khalice Jade * Til Kumari Sharma
Sushant Thapa * Orbindu Ganga

 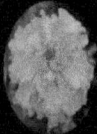 

| Innocence | Joy | Longing |
| Daisy | Marigold | Camellia |

The Poetry Posse 2025

Gail Weston Shazor * Albert Carasco * Hülya N. Yılmaz
Jackie Davis Allen * Caroline Nazareno * Mutawaf Shaheed
Alicja Maria Kuberska * Teresa E. Gallion * Noreen Snyder
Shareef Abdur – Rasheed * Swapna Behera * Eliza Segiet
Ashok K. Bhargava * Elizabeth Castillo * Kimberly Burnham
Tzemin Ition Tsai * William S. Peters, Sr.

The Year of the Poet XII
February 2025

Featured Global Poets

Shafkat Aziz Hajam * Frosina Tasevska
Muhammad Gaddafi Masoud * Karen Morrison

 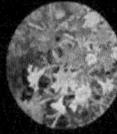 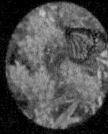

| Curiosity | Fear | Lonlines |
| Hibiscus | Minulus | Butterfly Weed |

The Poetry Posse 2025

Gail Weston Shazor * Albert Carasco * Hülya N. Yılmaz
Jackie Davis Allen * Caroline Nazareno * Mutawaf Shaheed
Alicja Maria Kuberska * Teresa E. Gallion * Noreen Snyder
Shareef Abdur – Rasheed * Swapna Behera * Eliza Segiet
Ashok K. Bhargava * Elizabeth Castillo * Kimberly Burnham
Tzemin Ition Tsai * William S. Peters, Sr.

The Year of the Poet XII
March 2025

Featured Global Poets

Deepak Kumar Dey * Binod Dawadi
Faleeha Hassan * Kapardeli Eftichia

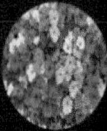  

| Frustration | Sorrow | Detrmination |
| Petunias | Purple Hyacinth | Amaryllis |

The Poetry Posse 2025

Gail Weston Shazor * Albert Carasco * Hülya N. Yılmaz
Jackie Davis Allen * Caroline Nazareno * Mutawaf Shaheed
Alicja Maria Kuberska * Teresa E. Gallion * Noreen Snyder
Shareef Abdur – Rasheed * Swapna Behera * Eliza Segiet
Ashok K. Bhargava * Elizabeth Castillo * Kimberly Burnham
Tzemin Ition Tsai * William S. Peters, Sr.

The Year of the Poet XII
April 2025

Featured Global Poets

Gopal Sinha * Taghrid Bou Merhi
Irma Kurti * Marlon Salem Gruezo

  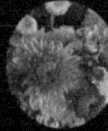

| Resilience | Self Doubt | Grief |
| Calendula | Centaury | Chrysanthemums |

The Poetry Posse 2025

Gail Weston Shazor * Albert Carasco * Hülya N. Yılmaz
Jackie Davis Allen * Caroline Nazareno * Mutawaf Shaheed
Alicja Maria Kuberska * Teresa E. Gallion * Noreen Snyder
Shareef Abdur – Rasheed * Swapna Behera * Eliza Segiet
Ashok K. Bhargava * Elizabeth Castillo * Kimberly Burnham
Tzemin Ition Tsai * William S. Peters, Sr.

Now Available

www.innerchildpress.com/the-year-of-the-poet

The Year of the Poet XII
May 2025

Featured Global Poets

**Swayam Prashant * Ngozi Olivia Osuoha
Kazimierz Burnat * Deepak Kumar Dey**

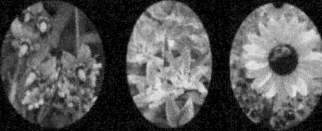

Bittersweetness   Empathy   Sadness
Bittersweetness   Lillies   Sunflowers

The Poetry Posse 2025

Gail Weston Shazor * Albert Carasco * Hülya N. Yılmaz
Jackie Davis Allen * Caroline Nazareno * Mutawaf Shaheed
Alicja Maria Kuberska * Teresa E. Gallion * Noreen Snyder
Shareef Abdur – Rasheed * Swapna Behera * Eliza Segiet
Ashok K. Bhargava * Elizabeth Castillo * Kimberly Burnham
Tzemin Ition Tsai * William S. Peters, Sr.

The Year of the Poet XII
June 2025

Featured Global Poets

Ayham Mahmoud Al-Abbad * Til Kumari Sharma
Michael Lee Johnson * Sylwia K. Malinowska

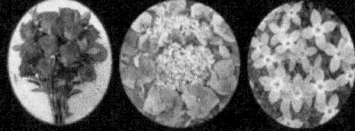

Love   Gratitude   Contentment
Red Roses   Blue Hydrangea   Azure Bluets

The Poetry Posse 2025

Gail Weston Shazor * Albert Carasco * Hülya N. Yılmaz
Jackie Davis Allen * Caroline Nazareno * Mutawaf Shaheed
Alicja Maria Kuberska * Teresa E. Gallion * Noreen Snyder
Shareef Abdur – Rasheed * Swapna Behera * Eliza Segiet
Ashok K. Bhargava * Elizabeth Castillo * Kimberly Burnham
Tzemin Ition Tsai * William S. Peters, Sr.

The Year of the Poet XII
July 2025

Featured Global Poets

Mennadi Farah * Aklima Ankhi
Niloy Rafiq * Petros Kyriakou Veloudas

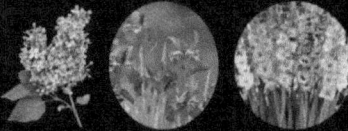

Nostalgia   Wisdom   Fearlessness
Lillaes   Purple Iris   Gladiolas

The Poetry Posse 2025

Gail Weston Shazor * Albert Carasco * Hülya N. Yılmaz
Jackie Davis Allen * Caroline Nazareno * Mutawaf Shaheed
Alicja Maria Kuberska * Teresa E. Gallion * Noreen Snyder
Shareef Abdur – Rasheed * Swapna Behera * Eliza Segiet
Ashok K. Bhargava * Elizabeth Castillo * Kimberly Burnham
Tzemin Ition Tsai * William S. Peters, Sr.

The Year of the Poet XII
August 2025

Featured Global Poets

Ivan Pozzoni * Ram Krishna Singh
Ibrahim Honjo * Kazimierz Burnat

Connection   Fulfillment   Hope
Sunflower   Lotus   Daffodils

The Poetry Posse 2025

Gail Weston Shazor * Albert Carasco * Hülya N. Yılmaz
Jackie Davis Allen * Caroline Nazareno * Mutawaf Shaheed
Alicja Maria Kuberska * Teresa E. Gallion * Noreen Snyder
Shareef Abdur – Rasheed * Swapna Behera * Eliza Segiet
Ashok K. Bhargava * Elizabeth Castillo * Kimberly Burnham
Tzemin Ition Tsai * William S. Peters, Sr.

Now Available

www.innerchildpress.com/the-year-of-the-poet

243

The Year of the Poet XII
September 2025

Featured Global Poets

Abeera Mirza * Shaswata Gangopadhyay
Shahid Abbas Shahid * Snežana Šolkotović

 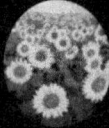 

Isolation   Empowerment   Confusion
Water Violet   Sunflower   Pink Larkspur

The Poetry Posse 2025

Gail Weston Shazor * Albert Carasco * Hülya N. Yılmaz
Jackie Davis Allen * Caroline Nazareno * Mutawaf Shaheed
Elizabeth Castillo * Teresa E. Gallion * Noreen Snyder
Ashok K. Bhargava * Swapna Behera * Eliza Segiet
Tzemin Ition Tsai * Alicja Maria Kuberska
Kimberly Burnham * William S. Peters, Sr.

The Year of the Poet XII
October 2025

Featured Global Poets

Фросина Тасевска * Tanja Ajtic
Jerome L. Duque * Priyanka Neogi

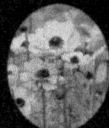 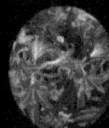 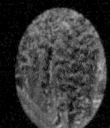

Anticipation   Pride   Regret
Anemone   Amaryllis   Purple Hyacinths

The Poetry Posse 2025

Gail Weston Shazor * Albert Carasco * Hülya N. Yılmaz
Jackie Davis Allen * Caroline Nazareno * Mutawaf Shaheed
Elizabeth Castillo * Teresa E. Gallion * Noreen Snyder
Ashok K. Bhargava * Swapna Behera * Eliza Segiet
Tzemin Ition Tsai * Alicja Maria Kuberska
Kimberly Burnham * William S. Peters, Sr.

The Year of the Poet XII
November 2025

Featured Global Poets

Zainul Husain * Robert Allen Goodrich Valderrama
Hong Ngoc Chau * D. Wahida Hussein

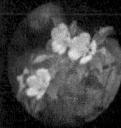 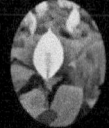 

Anxiety   Peacefulness   Grief
Columbine   Peace Lilly   Orchids

The Poetry Posse 2025

Gail Weston Shazor * Albert Carasco * Hülya N. Yılmaz
Jackie Davis Allen * Caroline Nazareno * Mutawaf Shaheed
Elizabeth Castillo * Teresa E. Gallion * Noreen Snyder
Ashok K. Bhargava * Swapna Behera * Eliza Segiet
Tzemin Ition Tsai * Alicja Maria Kuberska
Kimberly Burnham * William S. Peters, Sr.

The Year of the Poet XII
December 2025

Featured Global Poets

Elizabeth Cassidy * Neha Bhandarkar
Sajid Hussain * Mirjana Stefanicki Antonić

 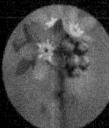 

Transcendence   Legacy   Satisfaction
Water Lily   Forget-me-nots   Daisies

The Poetry Posse 2025

Gail Weston Shazor * Albert Carasco * Hülya N. Yılmaz
Jackie Davis Allen * Caroline Nazareno * Mutawaf Shaheed
Elizabeth Castillo * Teresa E. Gallion * Noreen Snyder
Ashok K. Bhargava * Swapna Behera * Eliza Segiet
Tzemin Ition Tsai * Alicja Maria Kuberska
Kimberly Burnham * William S. Peters, Sr.

Now Available

www.innerchildpress.com/the-year-of-the-poet

and there is much, much more !

visit . . .

www.innerchildpress.com/antho
logies-sales-special.php

Also check out our Authors and
all the wonderful Books
Available at :

www.innerchildpress.com/autho
rs-pages

World Healing World Peace 2022

Poets for Humanity

Now Available

www.worldhealingworldpeacepoetry.com

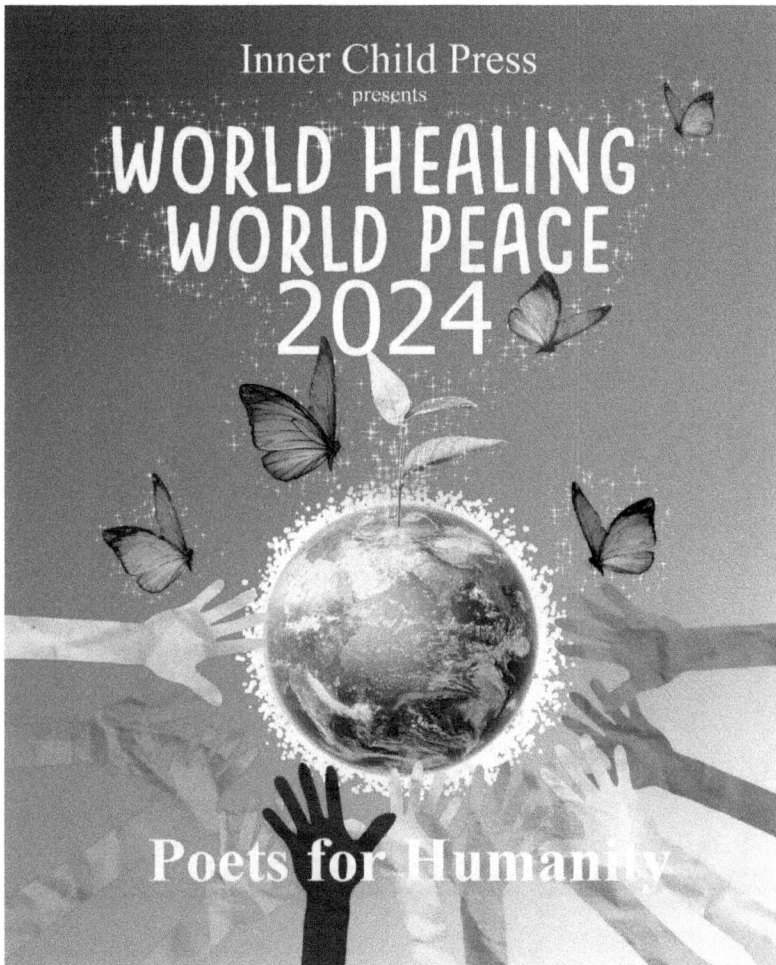

Inner Child Press
presents

WORLD HEALING
WORLD PEACE
2024

Poets for Humanity

Now Available

www.worldhealingworldpeacepoetry.com

World Healing World Peace
2020

Poets for Humanity

Now Available

www.worldhealingworldpeacepoetry.com

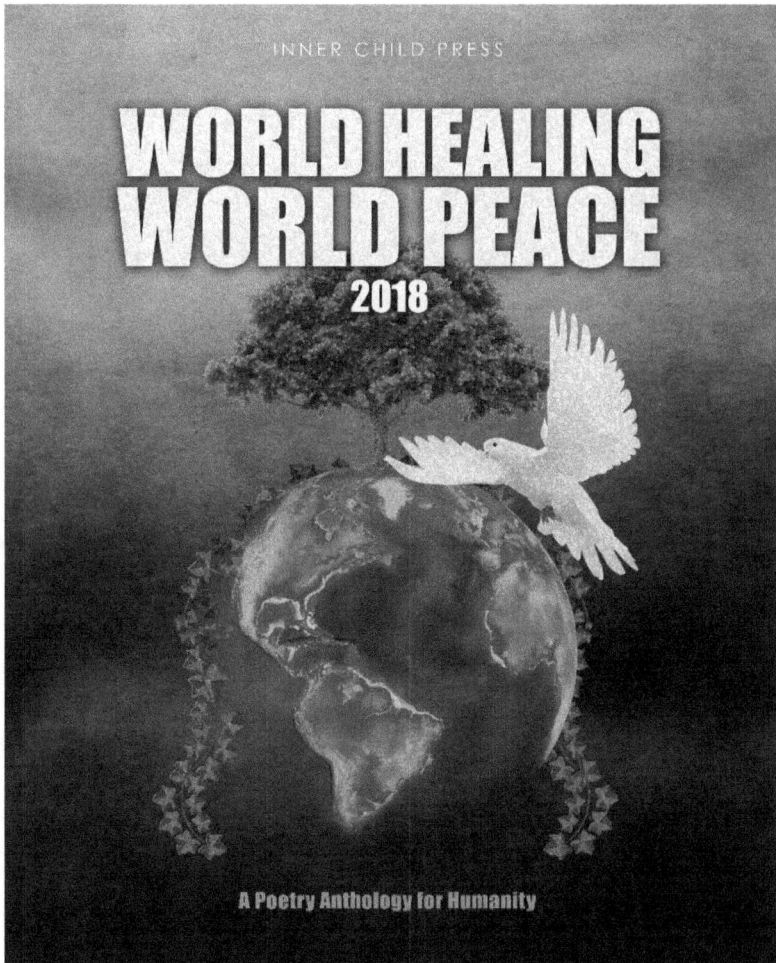

INNER CHILD PRESS

WORLD HEALING WORLD PEACE
2018

A Poetry Anthology for Humanity

Now Available

www.worldhealingworldpeacepoetry.com

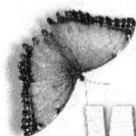

World Healing
World Peace

I support

www.worldhealingworldpeacepoetry.com

World Healing World Peace Poetry

i am a believer!

World Healing World Peace

2012, 2014, 2016, 2018,
2020, 2022, 2024

Now Available

www.worldhealingworldpeacepoetry.com

Inner Child Press International

'building bridges of cultural understanding'

Meet the Board of Directors

William S. Peters, Sr.
Chair Person
Founder
Inner Child Enterprises
Inner Child Press

Hülya N Yılmaz
Director
Editing Services
Co-Chair Person

Fahredin B. Shehu
Director
Cultural Affairs

Elizabeth E. Castillo
Director
Recording Secretary

De'Andre Hawthorne
Director
Performance Poetry

Gail Weston Shazor
Director
Anthologies

Kimberly Burnham
Director
Cultural Ambassador
Pacific Northwest
USA

Ashok K. Bhargava
Director
WIN Awards

Deborah Smart
Director
Publicity
Marketing

Khalice Jade
Director
Translation
Services

www.innerchildpress.com

252

Inner Child Press International

'building bridges of cultural understanding'

Meet our Cultural Ambassadors

Fahredin Shehu
Director of Cultural

Faleha Hassan
Iraq - USA

Elizabeth E. Castillo
Philippines

Antoinette Coleman
Chicago
Midwest USA

Ananda Nepali
Nepal - Tibet
Northern India

Kimberly Burnham
Pacific Southwest
USA

Alicja Kuberska
Poland
Eastern Europe

Swapna Behera
India
Southeast Asia

Kolade O. Freedom
Nigeria
West Africa

Monsif Beroual
Morocco
Northern Africa

Ashok K. Bhargava
Canada

Tzemin Ition Tsai
Republic of China
Greater China

Alicia M. Ramirez
Mexico
Central America

Christena AV Williams
Jamaica
Caribbean

Louise Hudon
Eastern Canada

Aziz Mountassir
Morocco
Northern Africa

Shureef Abdur-Rasheed
Southeastern USA

Laure Charazac
France
Western Europe

Mohammad Ikbal Harb
Lebanon
Middle East

**Mohamed Abdel
Aziz Shmeis**
Egypt
Middle East

Hilary Mainga
Kenya
Eastern Africa

Josephus R. Johnson
Liberia

Mennadi Farah
Algeria

www.innerchildpress.com

This Anthological Publication
is underwritten solely by

Inner Child Press International

Inner Child Press is a Publishing Company
Founded and Operated by Writers. Our
personal publishing experiences provides
us an intimate understanding of the
sometimes daunting challenges Writers,
New and Seasoned may face in the
Business of Publishing and Marketing
their Creative "Written Work".

For more Information

Inner Child Press International

www.innerchildpress.com

'building bridges of cultural understanding'
202 Wiltree Court, State College, Pennsylvania 16801

www.innerchildpress.com

This is our world . . .

~ fini ~

www.ingramcontent.com/pod-product-compliance
Lightning Source LLC
LaVergne TN
LVHW051041080426
835508LV00019B/1638